Rowing it
Alone

Rowing it
Alone

**One Woman's Extraordinary
Transatlantic Adventure**

DEBRA VEAL

ROBSON BOOKS

First published in Great Britain in 2002 by Robson Books, 64 Brewery Road, London, N7 9NT

A member of the Chrysalis Group plc

British Library Cataloguing in Publication Data
A catalogue record for this title is available from the British Library.

ISBN 1 86105 547 1

Typeset by SX Composing DTP, Rayleigh, Essex
Printed in Great Britain by Creative Print & Design (Wales), Ebbw Vale

Credits
Pictures: Grateful acknowledgement is made to *Express* newspapers, John Farndell, Chris Brandis and Mark Pepper for their kind permission to reproduce their images. Unless otherwise stated, photographs are courtesy of Debra Veal.
Grateful acknowledgement is made to EMI Music Publishing for their kind permission ro reproduce the New Radicals' lyrics.
Grateful aknowledgement is made to *The Times* for their kind permission to reproduce the article from 28/01/02. All drawings set at chapter openings are by Debra Veal.

Dedicated to
Robin Lynn Newbury

Dad, thank you for teaching me,
through your words and actions,
that in the face of adversity
it is still possible to
achieve your dreams.

Contents

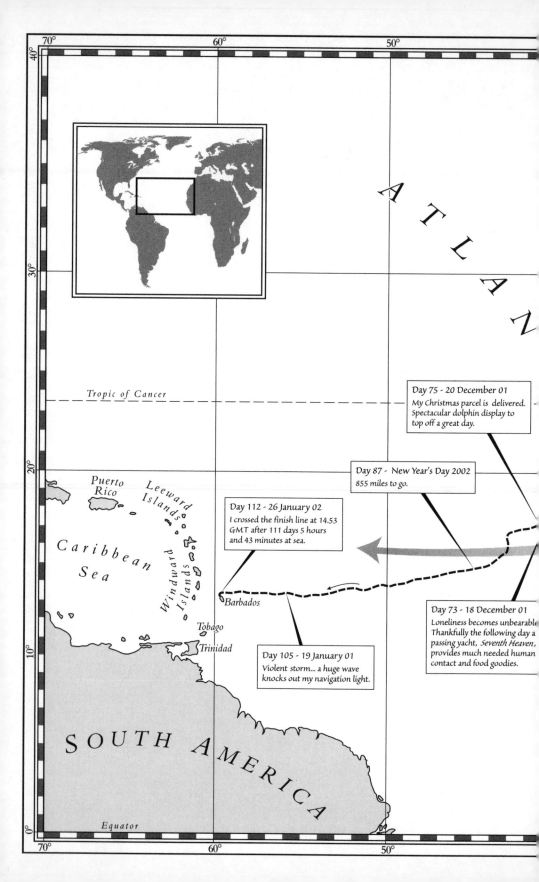

70° 60° 50°

40°

30°

A T L A N

Tropic of Cancer

20°

Day 75 - 20 December 01
My Christmas parcel is delivered.
Spectacular dolphin display to
top off a great day.

Day 87 - New Year's Day 2002
855 miles to go.

Puerto
Rico

*Leeward
Islands*

Day 112 - 26 January 02
I crossed the finish line at 14.53
GMT after 111 days 5 hours
and 43 minutes at sea.

*C a r i b b e a n
S e a*

*Windward
Islands*

Barbados

Day 73 - 18 December 01
Loneliness becomes unbearable
Thankfully the following day a
passing yacht, *Seventh Heaven*,
provides much needed human
contact and food goodies.

Tobago

Trinidad

Day 105 - 19 January 01
Violent storm... a huge wave
knocks out my navigation light.

10°

S O U T H   *A M E R I C A*

Equator

70° 60° 50°

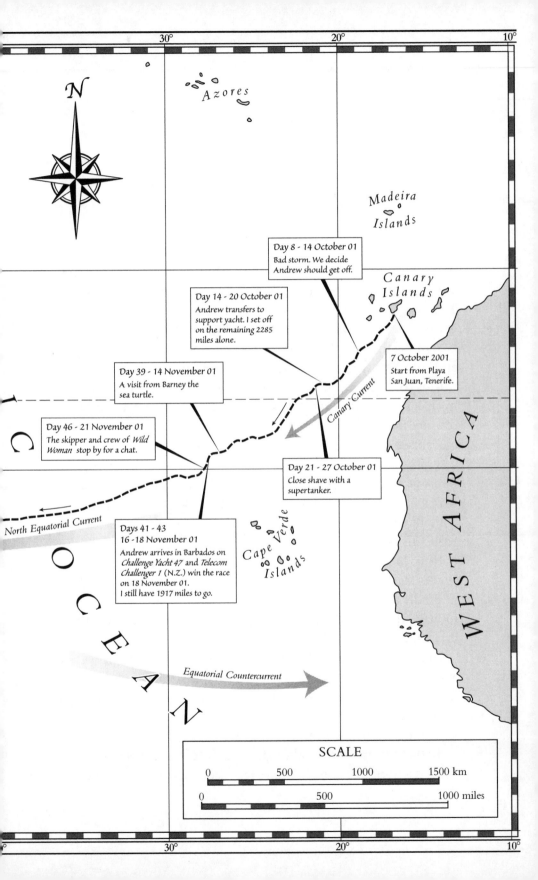

Acknowledgements

At no time when I was physically alone at sea did the *Troika Transatlantic* team of family, friends and supporters ever leave me. They were with me – motivating and supporting me through the harmonious times and the desperate times. A friend highlighted this beautifully through the words text to me. She wrote, 'I have laughed and cried with you all the way across the Atlantic.' I know this to be true of so many and feel blessed to have these wonderful people in my life. I'm proud to say that this 'solo transatlantic rower' definitely did not row solo! Sadly the extent of this team effort is rarely recognised or acknowledged and this has been especially true in the case of Andrew's contribution. It is therefore my great privilege to publicly acknowledge and thank Andrew and so many others who kept me going. You all got me to the other side of that big pond and without your help I would never have been given the opportunity to write this book. Thank you.

In particular I would like to thank Mum, Simon, Matt, Chris, Hayley, Leigh, Andrew, Jo and Pete for believing in me so whole-heartedly and for making my dream come true by being in Barbados to make that landfall moment the best of my life. It was worth the three-and-a-half month wait!

Huge thanks must also go to Leigh for creating a fantastic website and Jo and Pete for being friends who went well beyond the call of duty. Accumulatively, along with Hayley, you three spread the *Troika Transatlantic* story and somehow managed to rally supporters from all around the world.

To those supporters – although so many of us will never meet, this book is a tribute to you all. I have laughed, cried and been humbled through your tales. Thank you for keeping my oars in motion.

To Wendy Bray – thank you for teaching me how to write a book and for editing and re-editing every chapter. Thank you for respecting my desire to write the book in my own words and voice. But most importantly, thank you for your sensitivity. You have helped me put into words the hardest of issues and I'm not just talking about the obvious one. Your strength is a wonder but I now know where it comes from. You have taught me so much more than how to write a book.

To Kate Shaw at Gillon Aitken Associates, my incredibly patient and helpful literary agent, thank you for putting up with my endless questions!

To all at Robson Books, particularly Senior Editor Joanne Brooks, you have been great and your attention to detail has been immensely comforting.

To the best twin sister in the world – Hayley. What skills, intelligence and talents you have in abundance, not least for being able to persuade me that I loved it out there, even when I was crying hysterically and ringing to tell you that I was considering giving up! How did you do that? I am complete because you are actively part of my life.

Finally – Andrew – every word I have uttered to journalists and TV presenters about how much I respect the way you have handled this situation, and how much braver you are than me for having the courage to publicly admit your fears, is true. My love and admiration for you has only grown stronger for this unlikely adventure that we have found ourselves experiencing. The word 'inspirational' should be applied to you, not me.

Foreword by
Sir Chay Blyth CBE BEM

It's not often that one ordinary girl provides the inspiration for thousands by turning adversity into triumph and nightmares into dreams fulfilled. Least of all in front of a watching media world. But perhaps Debra Veal is not such an ordinary girl.

When Debra and husband Andrew first decided that they wanted to take part in the Ward Evans Atlantic Rowing Challenge we were absolutely delighted. Hayley, Debra's sister, already worked with us, making the plan something of a family affair, and Andrew and Debra were our first husband and wife team. I knew that this 'first' alone would make an inspirational race story. I could never have known just how inspirational.

Debra is a petite, determined and enthusiastic individual, yet I wondered if Debra's enthusiasm would be enough to enable her to make the tough crossing. But her determination assured me that she'd give it her best shot. After all she'd have the support of Andrew – a foot taller, strong, athletic, and with vast rowing experience – by her side.

They started the race well so the early news that Andrew was having difficulties was a shock. First reports told us that Andrew was struggling in the confined space and becoming increasingly nervous in the open sea. His fear of the ocean grew, heightened by lack of sleep because of his size. As his condition deteriorated, we realised that Andrew wasn't lacking bravery or power, but suffering from a very real phobia, rendering him useless in the boat, dashing hopes and threatening dreams.

Andrew and Debra faced a huge choice. They could both leave

their boat, *Troika Transatlantic*, and those dreams behind or leave Debra to carry on rowing solo. To Andrew's surprise Debra said that she had always intended to carry on by herself should Andrew be unable to. After much agony, reluctantly, and together, they made the decision that Debra should continue – alone.

So with Andrew's blessing, and more than a few thoughts of whether they would see each other again, Debra began her incredible voyage of discovery . . . but that's her tale to tell.

Debra not only rowed across the Atlantic solo, but into the editorials of national newspapers, the media spotlight and the hearts of thousands. She became the new-found heroine of the Atlantic.

Her story is a truly inspirational one.

Introduction

On a warm June afternoon in 1966, a young Scotsman stood on the beach of a little finishing port near Cape Cod, Massachusetts. In the foreground was a small wooden rowing boat. Beyond stretched the vastness of the North Atlantic Ocean.

Ninety-two days later, Chay Blyth and John Ridgeway rowed the *English Rose III* towards the rugged coastline of Ireland after an epic adventure into the unknown. At 26 years of age, Chay had successfully rowed the Atlantic, and this is where our story begins.

Three decades later, in celebration of his amazing Atlantic crossing, Chay Blyth had a madcap idea. At that time, more people had been to the moon than had rowed across the Atlantic, but, undeterred, Chay and his company, Challenge Business, created the 1997 Atlantic Rowing Race. It was the first ever rowing race across an ocean. Double-handed teams set out from Tenerife in identical 24-foot (7.3 metre) marine-plywood rowing boats, to compete on equal terms over a 2,900-nautical-mile voyage across the Atlantic Ocean to Barbados.

That year, as 60 adventurous souls set out across the Atlantic, two other adventurous souls came together for the first time. From the day I met my husband, Andrew Veal, I knew we had a lifetime of amazing experiences together ahead of us. We shared the same spirit of adventure and love of the outdoors. We vowed that in settling down together we would not settle for a life *lacking* in adventure.

The 1997 Atlantic Rowing Race had been intended as a one-off, but after its success Chay Blyth saw no reason to end the story there. An east-to-west race across the Atlantic was planned for every four years and we were determined to be on that start line in 2001.

So were a further 34 teams of competitors drawn from 13 countries, making it a truly international race.

Andrew and I were the only married team in what became the Ward Evans Atlantic Rowing Challenge, and the only mixed-sex team. We lined up against 32 double-handed men's teams and just one all-female team, off Playa San Juan Harbour, Tenerife on 7 October 2001. An adventure of vast proportions unfolded over the subsequent four months – perhaps not as we had planned but an epic adventure, for both of us, nonetheless.

Our story was originally documented through the diary entries published on our team website. It had been created to keep our friends, families and sponsors informed of our progress, but soon, via email and the internet, the story was being shared in all corners of the world.

Through sharing our lives we heard about others, via email and text messages: heart-rending stories that humbled, funny text messages that raised the spirit and stories of life experiences in their purest form. It was these supporters who encouraged me to turn the diary entries into a book. Their stories have become part of my story. They are included on the following pages.

This is not a book about rowing: it is a book about adventure – an adventure that was about so much more than the physical dipping of a pair of oars in and out of the water. It is about the adventure of life and love and the challenge of commitment. Commitment to a cause, to a dream and to each other.

Chapter 1

Change of Plan

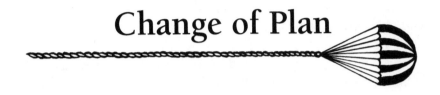

Mother Nature delivered another blow, her unrelenting waves slapping me across the face. I spat out the briny water and shook my head, trying to remove the stinging salt from my eyes. She had been a graceful companion as we'd rowed away from Tenerife a few hours earlier, giving us an awe-inspiring start to our race across the ocean. But now her anger – in the watery form of the Atlantic – was roused.

As the winds picked up and the waves became ferocious I began to see a nervousness in Andrew that I had not witnessed before. The waves were breaking over the boat and, although adrenaline prevented us from feeling tired, we felt helpless. It was almost dark; we had lost control of the boat and didn't know what to do to regain it. Andrew, too, looked lost. I wondered if this was the first time in his life that he couldn't find the answers he needed.

We were entering the acceleration zone, where all the winds that have funnelled around the Canary Islands reunite, and were having our first taste of what life on the ocean in a small wooden rowing boat was really going to be like. We struggled on through the night, as the stormy conditions enveloped us, refusing to acknowledge that our attempts were futile against such power. Without moonlight it was impossible to see and respond to the waves. They were intermittently twice the height of the boat, hitting us from all angles and threatening to capsize us. This was our first experience of such conditions. We had little knowledge of, or confidence in, the boat's reactions. Training off the coasts of England and Wales had ill-prepared us for what the Atlantic Ocean was now – literally – throwing at us.

By 2 a.m. we were exhausted and soaked to the skin, yet still rowing. Struggling to be heard above the waves, I shouted, 'Andrew, we're not getting anywhere!'

'Hmm.'

'We're just burning up the little energy supplies we have left.'

'But if we stop, the boat will spin side-on to the waves – we'll get even more of a hammering.'

'Not if we put a sea anchor out. What do you reckon?'

'I'll give anything a try at this stage.'

We had three different sizes of sea anchor on board, two of which we had been lent just prior to leaving the UK. We had not heard about the third type of anchor until we arrived in Tenerife. Some other competitors had told us about an extremely effective large parachute anchor that they had used during their sea trials to keep the boat from being blown backwards in strong headwinds or to keep the bow facing onto the waves in rough seas. With the words 'I wouldn't set out to sea without one' ringing in our ears, we duly set about having a para-anchor* delivered from Australia. It arrived within hours of our departure and now, only hours into the journey, we were seeking its assistance, but we had no experience of how to use it. The early hours of the morning, in the pitch black with waves breaking over the boat, was not a good time to be getting out the instruction manual.

As soon as we stopped rowing, *Troika Transatlantic* broached, making it difficult to work at the ropes. The boat was being thrown around and shunted along. All we could do was hang on. Anything to do with ropes and knots was supposed to be my department, but

*See glossary for a list of technical terms.

looking down into the hatch while fiddling with the knots immediately made me feel queasy.

We deployed the para-anchor with all 80 metres of rope. This was completely unnecessary, but as novices we didn't realise. We hoped the anchor would take hold in the water and turn the bow into the onslaught of waves. Wishful thinking. We obviously hadn't trimmed the boat sufficiently and now had far too much weight in the bow of the boat rather than at the stern. It was determined to hold us side-on to the waves.

Andrew was sick over the side, which raised my queasiness to a whole new level. I tried to focus on my task, hoping it would take my mind off the need to vomit. We stripped off our wet layers and crawled into the cabin, bucket positioned just outside the hatch. Seconds later I joined the vomit brigade! As we lay side by side in the cabin, there was no space to move.

'This is not my idea of a good time,' Andrew huffed.

With my stomach sore from retching I had to agree, but stayed silent, not wanting to sink our moods any lower. Andrew had hardly eaten all day. I was only slightly more nourished and was aware that we both needed food, but neither of us could stomach it. We were going to have to look after ourselves better if we were to get through the first few days.

The night was one long barrage of pounding waves, which allowed for little rest. The boat was designed to be self-righting but this worked only when the cabin hatch was closed, making a secure air pocket. Yet if we closed the hatch completely the cabin would become airtight and we would eventually run out of oxygen. So we spent the night with the hatch slightly ajar, each of us with a hand gripping one of the handles. When a big wave hit and the boat was rolled up on its side, we would quickly pull the handles in and down to secure the hatch. It was not conducive to a good night's sleep, but at the time we had no idea how far the boat could tip before it completely rolled.

Andrew woke, frustrated that we were still side-on to the waves and convinced that we were doing something wrong. He had found the night horrendous, imagining that each slapping wave against the side of the cabin was the cracking noise of *Troika Transatlantic* breaking up – while I found it comforting. It was a sound I knew and loved as a child. It reminded me of sleeping on my father's boat.

On the morning of Day Two, as light crept onto the horizon, we were able to survey the scene. It was apparent that conditions had not improved. Andrew was becoming paranoid, thinking we were the only crew caught in the rough conditions and that the other 34 teams must have gained hundreds of miles on us. We began to discuss the options, but not having any answers only increased Andrew's feelings of being out of control. I was optimistic and full of suggestions, but each one was greeted with an uncharacteristically negative response.

'I feel completely out of my depth,' Andrew commented unhappily. 'I didn't come out here to be thrown in all directions by the waves. I came out here to row and we aren't even able to do that in these conditions.'

'The guys from the '97 race told us that the first five days are the hardest,' I reminded him.

'I thought they said that getting to the start line was the hardest part!' Andrew snapped. 'Now it's the first five days as well?'

'It will get better,' I said. 'After five days the seasickness will have passed, we'll have found our sea legs and we'll be out of the acceleration zone.'

I really hoped this was true, particularly the bit about the sea legs. At six foot five, Andrew was far too big for the boat and was constantly colliding with everything. He was going to hurt either himself or *Troika*!

Andrew was quiet for the next few hours, obviously thinking everything through. When he finally responded he said, 'OK, let's give it a go for five days, then we'll see how we feel.'

To my great relief his mood lifted, and he seemed brighter for a while. We gave up trying to fight our way across the waves and altered our course to run with them. This produced a whole new set of frustrations. The boat would not stay on the line of the waves and continuously spun off to one side or the other. Believing there was an answer, and with my optimism still buoyant, I set up a bridle around the stern of the boat to trail a drogue behind us. It slowed us down a little, but helped keep the vessel straight. I was desperate to do anything that would ease Andrew's frustrations with the boat's performance and the general situation.

By evening Andrew was low again and nothing I did or said seemed to make any difference. Finally he agreed that it might help him to talk to his friend Pete King, a key member of our support team, on the satellite phone. Pete had access, via the Internet, to information on the progress of the other crews. I hoped it would put Andrew's mind at rest to discover that we weren't the only ones stuck in the rough conditions.

Andrew started by asking Pete where we were in the race.

'It's hard to tell,' Pete explained, 'because everyone is polling at different times and some are not polling at all.'

Andrew looked frustrated and replied, 'Well, roughly where are we in the fleet – at the front, middle or back?'

Pete explained that the fleet had now split into three groups: a leading group, followed by a chasing pack and a final group bringing up the rear.

'You're in the middle of the chasing pack,' he said, 'in about twentieth place'.

Pete tried to reassure us by explaining that the calculations were based on the distance remaining to Barbados. The crews that had elected to take a straight route had initially taken the lead as they were literally heading straight towards the island. Those who were attempting to pick up the stronger trade winds had focused on heading south, so had not significantly reduced the distance between themselves and Barbados.

The call certainly reduced our stress levels. It was reassuring to know that everyone was being delayed by the weather conditions, but disappointing to discover that we had slipped from fourth place in the race on Day One to twentieth place. But we couldn't remain disappointed for long. We had bigger concerns: would Andrew last another day?

The seasickness did not return after that first night, but Andrew still hadn't eaten. On Day Three, after another sleepless night, I became increasingly concerned about lack of food and sleep and the effect that this was having on Andrew's ability to think straight. My emotions were in complete turmoil. I was desperately worried about Andrew. But the sun shone, I was surfing down waves and absolutely loving life at sea. It was hard to believe we could feel so differently about the same experience.

Later, I sat in the foot well, cooking lunch, and watched Andrew rowing on.

'This is great, isn't it?' I beamed happily.

No reply from Andrew. I continued. 'Out here on the ocean, just the two of us, all on our own.'

His face dropped as he finally replied, 'If only I could start to see it that way, this would all be so much more enjoyable.'

I could see the sadness in his eyes. He wanted so badly to be enjoying it.

'If I just didn't feel so scared all the time . . .'

I couldn't begin to imagine how it must feel to be as disillusioned and frightened as he was, when I found such joy in our surroundings.

It was such a shock for both of us to discover his hidden fear of being in a small boat on the ocean. There had been no evidence to suggest that there might be a problem in our sea trials off the coast of Britain. But the rough conditions of the wider Atlantic were altogether different. Without a view of a coastline and with thousands of miles to go, Andrew's very real fear became apparent. He seemed open to talk about it, and we hoped that would help.

'So what exactly are you scared of?' I asked tentatively.

'Everything – but nothing in particular. I can't pick one thing and say what it is. I wish I could, because maybe then we could find a solution.' As ever, he wanted to 'fix it'.

'But look at the alternatives,' I tried. 'If you give up, you'll have to go back to commuting into London every day on the tube, which you hate. It'll be cold, and you'll have nothing to look forward to.'

I was half-joking and half-hoping I'd provide reassurance.

'I know,' said Andrew. 'I've been thinking about that. But frankly, with the way I feel right now, anything would be better than being here. At our current rate I've calculated that it will take us nearer a hundred and fifty days than fifty days. I can't cope with being out here for that long.'

We tried to break down the fear into specific problems and how we could combat them. There had to be a solution to each one. I had majored in outdoor education at university and remembered a lecture on 'fear thresholds'. Something about a pyramid – if only I could remember the details. I called my twin Hayley and asked her to track down Mike Bartle, my former university lecturer. He had studied the psychology underlying Andrew's fear – and he had given the pyramid lecture. I was convinced he would have the answer. We were desperate to live our dream of rowing across the Atlantic together and were determined to find a way. But Mike could not be reached. He did not respond to Hayley's emails and appeared to have left De Montfort University. Our questions remained unanswered.

On the evening of the third day, the conditions calmed somewhat. We decided to row together through the night to make up some more mileage and keep morale high. Our long chats in the afternoon had helped and Andrew seemed more relaxed.

That night was our first clear night. The stars were breathtaking. I was charmed by everything above or on the ocean. The phosphorescence beneath the surface spun and whirled around our oars, like tiny sparkling fairies, as we pulled them through the dark water. I was mesmerised by this magical place.

By 3 a.m. we were exhausted, so we began singing 'Jerusalem', 'I Vow to Thee My Country' and 'American Pie' at the top of our voices in an effort to stay awake. Andrew's 'flexible' approach to the selection of musical keys only added to our amusement! To be fair, he was the only one who could remember the words. Singing became a huge morale booster, but, as we knew the words of only three songs, the repetition became a bit wearing by 6 a.m.! But that was how we had always dreamed it would be – laughing and smiling, enjoying our adventure together and united in our goal. I had glimpsed what that fulfilment could be like and longed for more.

By the end of Day Five there had been moments of joy, but little had changed in Andrew's mind. We felt it was only right to keep our supporters informed of our progress, but told only our closest friends and family members the whole story. Instead we hinted at our dilemma in a humorous way.

> **Web diary entry:**
> After our recent rather matter-of-fact updates we thought it was about time that we shared some of our personal feelings of life on board *Troika Transatlantic* with you.
>   In short, Debra is absolutely loving it, to the extent that Andrew suspects she must have been a dolphin in a former life-time. On the other hand Andrew's previous incarnations probably don't include anything other than a fish eagle (happy to dip his talons in the water from time to time but prefers to sleep in the trees!).
>   Comfort is a challenge, as the person who designed the boat was clearly thinking about someone more of Debra's size than Andrew's. This had led to a good amount of nautical language on Andrew's part and growling which is definitely not all coming from the ship's bear (Woody Aged 3).

Picking up on the underlying problem, the Challenge Business – the race organisers – sent one of the support yachts to check up on us. They were on their way back to Tenerife with the crew of the *Dartmothian* – another team from my home county of Devon – and would not be able to return again for another week. We had been told that one of the *Dartmothian* rowers had been suffering with similar anxiety problems to Andrew and had elected to get off. His team-mate had continued alone but had eventually given up too. We were disappointed for them, although for Andrew the news was, strangely, something of a boost. He had believed that he was the only one finding it hard. Hearing that others had already dropped out gave him the motivational drive he needed. The support yacht crew half expected us to give up and climb aboard, but we hadn't lost hope completely. We still believed that we would work it all out and that we would make it – together.

So many sceptics had predicted that being confined to a small rowing boat for so long would damage our marriage, but they could not have been more wrong. Being under such pressure, in a stressful situation with no escape from one another, actually bound us closer together. So much closer that it was sometimes a little too tempting to sit and chat over a romantic boil-in-the-bag meal or abandon rowing altogether and get into the cabin! We talked for hours about moving house: where we would move to, and the features we'd like our dream family home to have. We imagined what it would be like to start a family, which names we would choose and where our children might go to school. We reminisced about the past and talked excitedly about the future and all it might hold for us.

Some days were better than others for Andrew – days full of awesome sightings of dolphins and turtles, evenings spent singing as we rowed under the stars. But he just couldn't shake the conviction that every thud of a rope or slap of a wave against the side of the boat was something cracking or breaking into pieces.

After a week, lack of sleep and food were causing him real anxiety problems. We discovered some antianxiety drugs in the first-aid pack, but they seemed such an extreme course of action. Were drugs really appropriate? We decided to call Sian, the race medic, for some much-needed advice.

'Do you feel stressed, scared or anxious?' asked Sian.

'All three!' was Andrew's brave admission.

They talked through his symptoms in more detail and Andrew asked about the side effects of taking such a drug.

'So is it appropriate for me to take them, with the symptoms I've described?'

Sian was certain. 'Absolutely,' she said.

The tablets immediately made a significant difference, taking the edge off Andrew's fear and allowing him to gain a calmer view of his situation. We both started to feel optimistic and really believed that we could beat this thing. But Day Eight was the big turning point from which there would be no way back.

Andrew spent the day trying to mend a leaky pump attached to the water maker. He grew more despondent as the hours passed, convinced that he was making the leak worse. He had lost confidence in his abilities and was increasingly self-deprecating. I had never seen this side of his generally stoical and optimistic character before. Perhaps he hadn't, either. He was certainly not used to being in a situation where he was unable to thrive on challenges. His frustration continued to build.

By the end of that evening, heavy rain had begun to fall and the first signs of a storm were evident. I pulled on my Musto waterproofs and crawled through the hatch for my evening shift while Andrew rested in the cabin. I was uncomfortable with the thunder and lightning, but was determined to make the most of the fact that the heavy rain appeared to have flattened the surface of the water. The sheet lightning flashed out of the darkness, violently lighting up my 360-degree water horizon, and set my heart pounding. The low groan of distant thunder sounded like an animal in pain, putting me on edge in the tense moments before the inevitable crescendo. When the thunder finally crashed and the lightning ricocheted across the surface of the water, the noise vibrated in my lungs, and left me cowering in the fleecy lining of my upturned collar.

At the end of my two-hour shift, I crawled along the deck and sat outside the hatch. Not wanting to let the rain into the cabin, I opened it only slightly. I shouted over the sound of the rain drumming on the roof of the cabin, 'Andrew, it's your turn!'

Andrew didn't move. I wondered if maybe he hadn't heard me.

'Andrew!' Still nothing. I tried some reassurance.

'It's not that bad out here if you put your Mustos on. It probably sounds worse than it is in the cabin with the noise of the rain hitting the plywood.'

He still didn't respond, but, after the day he'd had, I figured that he probably needed a bit more encouragement.

'Why don't you put the headphones on under your hood and listen to some music while you row?' Nothing. 'Andrew?'

Still only slightly concerned, I stuck my head in further, and was shocked by what I saw. Andrew had curled his massive frame into the foetal position. He was groaning as if in pain and shaking violently from head to toe. He was obviously terrified. I had tried encouraging, supporting and being there for him, but it just was not helping. I wondered if maybe I should try being firm.

'Andrew, I need your help,' I pleaded – and then, with an irony I couldn't have appreciated at the time: 'I can't row this boat to Barbados on my own. We're a team. We have to work together.'

I watched him for a moment, his body still shaking, numb and unresponsive. I knew he wouldn't make it.

'Well, if you aren't going to help, I guess I'll have to do it on my own.'

It was an unnecessary and low remark, made to force him into action. But it didn't.

There was nothing else I could do: I returned to the oars for another two-hour shift, filled with frustration.

Why couldn't Andrew love it out here? I wanted to shout at him to snap out of it and pull himself together, even though deep down I knew he couldn't. I knew, too, that fear can't simply be clicked on and off like a switch. Seeing the person I love in such anguish was unbearable. I felt so terribly sad that he had struggled so far and that I was unable to make it better for him.

Two hours later nothing had changed, except that I was now exhausted. I stripped off my sopping clothes and stuffed them into a bin liner, and crawled into the cabin next to Andrew. There was no point trying to talk. He had not responded for hours. I realised it would be better to wait until we had both rested.

I woke at 5.30 a.m. and found Andrew lying on his back, staring at the ceiling of the cabin with wide eyes. It was hard to believe that I was looking at the same person who had been curled in a ball just a few hours earlier. There was a serenity about him, almost a peacefulness. Something had changed.

'I can't go on.' His voice was calm and controlled. He sounded as if he had been considering his decision all night, but as he said the words I watched a tear roll down the side of his face. I realised in that moment that he had stopped fighting the fear and had finally given in. That was the source of his peacefulness.

'It's OK,' I said softly. 'I know.' I had known from the minute I had stuck my head through the hatch the previous night and had seen Andrew in a place where he should never had been – way out beyond his fear threshold. I saw no reason to tell him that.

It was the right decision – the only decision. We had to get him off the boat. I understood his tears of frustration. He had accepted that he had to give up on his dream and it was devastating for him. I longed to take away his pain. Such a big decision wasn't going to be an easy one to live with.

We lay holding each other for what seemed like hours and talked through the details. It was at this point that we discussed the option of me continuing alone.

'You realise that if you give up I would like to continue solo?'

He hadn't!

I explained that I thought I had mentioned it before we left England. I had presumed that, if either of us had to drop out, the other would give it a go alone. It was something I had been thinking about for years, since reading the story of a solo competitor in the 1997 Atlantic Rowing Race. John Searson, a meteorologist from

Guernsey, had continued solo after his partner was forced to retire because of a serious back injury. John knew that by continuing alone he would be disqualified from the race, but he was determined to complete the challenge. He did so in style, beating many of the double-handed crews across the finish line. I was so inspired after reading extracts from John's email diary that I decided then and there that if Andrew were injured I would continue the journey alone.

I had evidently not shared my decision with Andrew. Because of what he'd been through, Andrew was immediately concerned for my safety. So much so that his instant response was, 'Well then I can't get off. I'll stay with you.' But we both knew that was not an option. He was trapped in an impossible situation. Andrew couldn't possibly continue on board *Troika Transatlantic*, but if he got off and I continued alone, there was much at stake. Yet Andrew would never be so arrogant as to assume that he had the right to 'order' me to give up with him. His respect for me is too great for that and it was obvious to him just how happy I was at sea. He had perceived a confidence and assurance in me, more so than he had ever witnessed before. Determination seemed to exude from my very core and he wanted to support and foster that determination wholeheartedly.

So we went through the risks one by one of my continuing alone, as we both felt the need to be clear about what the emergency procedures would be. I knew Andrew well enough to know he would have to work through all the details before he could feel comfortable with the situation.

'With only you on board, you can't possibly keep a 24-hour look-out. You could so easily be mown down by a tanker.' He was right. This was one of the greatest risks I faced. I had to sleep at some time.

'I know. But I can take precautions. I'll only sleep for a maximum of 30 minutes at a time. I can get up and scan the horizon. I'll keep a flare right by the hatch so I can set off a signal quickly and I'll keep the VHF charged so that I can hail boats. The chances of us both being on the same patch of water at exactly the same time must be pretty slim.'

He continued, 'What if you get washed overboard? No one would know you were in the water and you wouldn't be able to raise the alarm.'

'But this could happen with us both on board. I could be washed overboard at night at the start of a two-hour watch. By the time you awoke two hours later I would be long gone.'

'Then you must promise me that you will always wear your safety harness and keep your lifeline clipped onto the boat.'

Then one factor that reassured both of us was that I was carrying a satellite phone. We would be able to call each other; I could call him during the tough times and if things got really bad I could always call for assistance. It also meant he could still be actively involved in assisting my progress across the Atlantic by providing me with navigation and meteorological advice and the emotional and moral support I was bound to need, allowing us still to be a team, even though we would be thousands of miles apart. The satellite phone could also receive text messages from anyone, anywhere in the world, who had Internet access. A link from the *Troika Transatlantic* website to the satellite phone company's website meant I would be able to receive a constant flow of encouraging and inspiring messages, not to mention useful information.

While Andrew had many concerns about my safety, I was equally concerned for him. Would people rush to accuse him of abandoning his wife at sea? What if the press decided to run with the story? I realised that, in choosing to go on alone, I was putting Andrew in a potentially humiliating and embarrassing situation and that he would need support from me.

Many hours later, we had discussed all the pros and cons of me continuing alone. There were certainly many cons but the fact was, deep down, Andrew knew I could do it. He had seen how capable and at one with the elements I had been on board *Troika* for the past week. Yes, there were risks, many of which were beyond our control, but you don't sign up to row across the Atlantic without expecting there to be a fair amount of risk involved. The level of risk had simply risen.

We knew Andrew would be fine on the Challenge Business support yacht. He'd spent time on yachts before. There's nothing quite like having 72 feet of steel hull under you to boost confidence levels.

As for me, the truth was I had no idea whether I would be able to cope on my own. As an identical twin, I had never spent a day alone in my life, but I knew I had to try. Maritime law stipulated that if we both got off *Troika Transatlantic*, she would have to be burned at sea in order to prevent her from becoming a floating hazard to other shipping. We had spent four years of our lives and a considerable amount of money preparing for life on the boat – we didn't want her to meet such a fate. But if I couldn't cope with being alone, I could always call the support yacht back to get me!

With our decision made, we called our support team – my sister Hayley, her husband Leigh and our friends Pete and Joanna – to discuss it with them. They were as loyal as ever and made constructive suggestions. Hayley, having worked for the Challenge Business, was able to predict what the issues would be. She was keen to establish whether my safety cover and insurance would still be valid, if the Spanish authorities would provide emergency assistance if required, and to what extent the safety yachts would provide backup cover in the light of *Troika Transatlantic* being disqualified from the race.

Then came the official call to Teresa Evans, the race manager, to inform her of our decision. I was concerned about the 'official' response, and wondered whether they would let me carry on alone. In fact their response was overwhelmingly positive. They were 100 per cent supportive. She confirmed that, in having Andrew taken off the rowing boat and onto the support yacht, we would be disqualified from the Ward Evans Atlantic Rowing Challenge. The race rules state that outside assistance is strictly forbidden and immediately results in disqualification. However, she also confirmed that Challenge Business would continue to provide me with the best possible safety cover, assuming I did not fall too far behind the rest of the competitors. Finally, she told us that we were the third boat to have one crew member drop out, and that two further crews had turned back to Tenerife and restarted.

The following days were busy and constructive. Although Andrew was worried for my safety, he didn't want to stop me fulfilling my dream, so threw himself wholeheartedly into making the boat as safe as possible for me. The steering system needed improving, so that I could access the cleats with ease from my central rowing position, and the weight had to be redistributed to the stern to prevent the boat turning side-on to the waves.

While we worked, we discussed how the situation would look to the outside world. I shared my concern that people would label Andrew a bad husband for 'abandoning' me, and felt sure that the situation would be misunderstood. It might be thought that the race had caused a rift between us. Or even that we had fallen out and gone our separate ways. Our best defence would be to tell the story as it really was.

A few days before the safety yacht was due to arrive to pick Andrew up, we put in a phone call to John Searson, the solo rower from 1997. He was full of good advice about how to trim the boat, and, being ever the helpful meteorologist, gave us the latest weather forecast. We were at a very similar location in the Atlantic to where John had continued solo and we discussed the best route. He had taken 59 days to cross from Tenerife to Barbados in 1997 – a phenomenal feat.

'I can't tell you it will be OK and to go for it,' John cautioned. 'That decision has to be yours.'

I wasn't looking for advice on how to make the decision – it had already been made. Wild horses wouldn't have stopped me going on! But I understood the wisdom of what John had said.

By Day Thirteen we had secured, fixed and rearranged everything that would make life safer and easier for me as I continued solo. Little rowing had been achieved. The waiting game began.

From the dawn of Day Fourteen we were on the lookout for the distinctive pale-yellow sails of *Challenge Yacht 24* on the horizon. An old friend from Devon, Jonathan Crawford, was skippering *Yacht 24* and I looked forward to seeing him. I was keen to keep rowing while we waited, despite the fact that it took us away from the yacht, as I still had a further 2,300 miles to go!

The mood was a mixture of sadness and excitement for both of us. Andrew was very pleased to be getting off *Troika Transatlantic* and I was excited about my new solo adventure – but we both hated the thought of being apart. At times Andrew seemed distant. The emotional battle must have been tough for him to deal with, and I couldn't decide which of my emotions was dominating – the enthusiasm of embarking on my new solo adventure, the sadness of being separated from Andrew or the relief of knowing that he was finally going to be safe and well. At least I didn't have fear or pressure to add to the list. I wasn't at all scared at the thought of being on my own in the middle of an ocean and didn't feel any particular pressure to succeed.

We first spotted the yacht at 1 p.m. Trying to find a rowing boat in the Atlantic is like spotting the proverbial needle in a haystack. Even when a yacht is only a mile away, a rowing boat is almost impossible to find, as it is constantly lost among the waves. It took the crew a further two hours until 3 p.m. to locate us. We finally made radio contact on the VHF and Andrew and I were then left with twenty minutes together before they would draw alongside. It was time to say our goodbyes.

Andrew sat outside the cabin, with his little bag packed, all ready to go. 'Just remember,' he assured me, 'if it doesn't work out, or if anything happens, we'll be right back to get you.'

'I know. I'll probably hate being on my own and we'll be back together in two days' time, but I've got to try. I'll always wonder "what if?" if I don't give it a go.'

'You will stay clipped in, won't you?'

'Yep.'

Andrew gave me a big hug. 'I'm going to miss you,' he muffled, his face buried into my hair.

'I'll miss you too.'

We held each other and cried. Andrew's anguish was obvious: 'I don't want to leave you now.'

'I don't want you to either, but it's for the best.'

There was something rather ominous about watching the Challenge yacht gliding slowly through the water towards us, its yellow sail apparently growing larger. It looked like the fin of a giant shark. This, I mused, was the thing that was going to be responsible for taking my husband away from me.

I felt really rather calm. Perhaps it was because we'd had a whole week to prepare us for the moment or, maybe, I had mentally prepared myself for the possibility four years before. During the weekend courses on ocean navigation and meteorology, I would say to myself, 'Now listen carefully, Debra, because if anything happens to Andrew you will need to be able to do this on your own.'

I felt strongly that everything was going to be OK and was excited at the prospect of spending many more weeks out on the ocean I had instantly fallen in love with as we'd left Tenerife.

'*Troika Transatlantic*, *Troika Transatlantic*, *Troika Transatlantic*, this is *Challenge 24*, *Challenge 24*, *Challenge 24*. Over.'

I instantly recognised the dulcet Irish tones of my old friend Jonathan Crawford. The yacht lined up right next to us, but it was still easier to hear each other if we talked through the VHF.

Andrew replied, '*Challenge 24*, this is *Troika Transatlantic*. Go ahead.'

'Hi, guys. We'll get the tender inflated and launched, then one of us will row over and pick you up. If you don't mind, Debra, we'd like you to come on board for a short time too, so that we can discuss some safety issues.'

I had been half expecting this, but didn't really want to leave the boat and climb aboard the yacht. The Challenge Business needed me to sign a declaration to cover liabilities. I also knew they had my best interests at heart.

It felt strange climbing aboard and having a comparatively solid and stable platform under my feet. I immediately felt uncomfortable and found it hard to walk. I looked back longingly at *Troika* and couldn't wait to get back to her. She looked so small, floating on her own among so much sky and sea – a small speck in such empty vastness. I couldn't believe how much the waves were tossing her around. We had got used to the motion and didn't realise how dramatic it was until we looked on her from afar.

Andrew and I sat down with Jonathan in the galley and talked through the problems Andrew had been having. Then we discussed how I would cope on my own. I just didn't know, and there was no point claiming otherwise. We could give Jonathan only an outline of our plans to ensure I would be safe.

'I'm going to make safety my number-one priority, obviously,' I explained. 'I'll stay clipped into my harness if it's rough and always at night.'

'We have that policy on the Challenge yachts – it's a good one to stick to,' said Jonathan. 'You have to remember that, if a wave washes you overboard, the wind would push the boat away faster than you could swim after it.'

'I realise that. I've got a flare and the EPIRB just inside the cabin hatch and we've moved the life raft to the foot well so that it's on deck and accessible.'

Jonathan seemed reassured. 'It sounds like you've thought this through carefully and logically.'

'We have.' I nodded. 'We feel certain we're doing what's best for both of us. I wouldn't be so bold as to say I'm going to make it all the way to Barbados – but I really want to give it a go.'

Jonathan smiled, 'I'm sure you'll do great, Debs, but, if you don't, just let Teresa know and we'll be right back.'

He grinned at an afterthought. 'We've got a DVD player on board, hot showers, stereo, proper food and all the mod cons, so we can look after you well if you do decide to give up.'

The grin widened. 'Don't tempt me, Jon!'

I wasn't tempted, but I was pleased that Andrew would get to enjoy those things. I knew Jonathan would look out for him. The sight of Andrew looking so relaxed was a great relief. The shadow of fear in his eyes had already lifted and the muscles of his face, tightened by stress, had relaxed.

As *Troika* was placed at the back of the rowing fleet, assisting us meant that the Challenge yacht needed to steam forward to catch up with the bulk of the rowing boats. They weren't able to take Andrew back to Tenerife. We knew he would get to arrive in Barbados by sea after all, an achievement in its own right, and one subsequently overlooked by Andrew's critics. Andrew was told that after a day resting he would be integrated into the crew watch rotation and become part of the race safety team. He was looking forward to it, now that his fear had dissipated.

I just didn't feel right on the yacht. Something about the way the tons of steel moved heavily through the water was making me feel queasy. The motion just wasn't the same. I had to get off before I was sick. I couldn't wait to get back on *Troika* and took that desire as confirmation that I had made the right decision. Once the declaration forms were written and signed, I was eager to begin my new adventure.

Up on deck, the atmosphere was light and happy, as I said my goodbyes to the crew. They teased Andrew that it was his turn to cook that night and he agreed to the challenge. I gave him a big hug and he whispered 'Good luck' in my ear. We had said everything we needed to say. It was time.

I climbed over the rail and lowered myself into the tender, while one of the crew steadied it, holding onto the side of the hull. We cast off and then we were on our way back towards my beautiful *Troika*. I looked straight ahead. There was no turning back now. My mind was made up.

Those first moments back on board *Troika* – alone – felt right. I was surprised by how little fear I felt, but the Atlantic had been good to me and I was yet to experience the ocean in a really bad mood.

I was bursting with anticipation and full of confidence.

Andrew stood by the Challenge yacht mast, waving to me with a big smile on his face. I smiled back, happy that he was safe. But, as I watched him sailing slowly into the distance, niggling doubts gnawed at my happiness. What if something went wrong? What if there was an accident or the elements turned against me?

I might never see Andrew again.

Chapter 2

Beginnings

I experienced Henley Royal Regatta for the first time in 1997, a month after I had left De Montfort University, Bedford. The sunny days were long, the glasses of Pimm's even longer. I didn't know it then, but Henley '97 was to be a very special week.

My friends Charlie and Joanna, both members of Thames Tradesmen Rowing Club, had hired an eight-berth boat for the week and moored it alongside the racecourse. The boat was 'party central' for the duration. As we stood in the boating area at the end of the racecourse, Charlie's phone rang.

'It's for you!' she said, swiftly handing me the phone. It was my dad. His voice was full of emotion and I immediately panicked. Dad had been having chemotherapy for two years, so I naturally assumed the worst.

'What's wrong, Dad?'

He was quick to reassure me: 'Nothing's wrong, darling. In fact it's quite the opposite. I've just had a phone call from your lecturer at Bedford. Your degree result is through. You got a first!'

With his voice cracking with pride, Dad outlined the details, sent his love, and rang off, leaving me to celebrate.

'I got a first!' I shouted at Charlie, everyone, no one in particular.

Much leaping about followed as I repeated the unbelievable over and over, as if trying to convince myself.

For so long I had been labelled as 'a sporty and arty girl' who had little academic ability. Now my critics had been proved wrong. It was time to celebrate.

The rowing crew we had been waiting for when I heard the news had lost their race, and were also in need of a drink.

That night in a crowded salon area of the party boat, I was still grinning in celebration when one of the rowers from the crew that lost entered and sat opposite me. I'd always believed 'love at first sight' to be another myth hatched by fifteenth-century Renaissance poets, but perhaps they were on to something, after all. I soon dismissed my over-the-top romantic notions as nothing more than a silly feeling probably induced by the heady mix of first-class degree results and champagne.

The rower later worked his way round to my side of the table to introduce himself. How ironic, looking back, that I first met Andrew Veal on a boat! The chemistry between us was instant, but as we talked, I began to feel that maybe I had met the right person at the wrong time. I was in and spend some time being single. I was about to begin my teaching career in Devon and was full of new and exciting plans. Most importantly, I wanted to be at home for Dad, as I'd not been able to spend much time with him since he'd received his diagnosis.

I had been at university when I was told he had cancer. One afternoon during my second year, I received a phone call from my twin sister, Hayley. She sounded shaky, apprehensive. Hayley asked if I had spoken to Mum. I said I hadn't, and asked, 'What about?'

There was a moment's pause.

'This is going to sound much worse than it actually is but – it's Dad. He's got cancer.'

I heard myself shout 'No!' as Hayley continued talking, trying to explain and reassure me at the same time. But I was hysterical. I couldn't hear her. My pulse banged in my temples as my temperature soared and tears flowed. It couldn't be true. Dad was an invincible dad – a happy, smiling, invincible dad. He was never ill. He couldn't possibly die.

Hayley tried to calm me down, encouraging me to believe that death was not inevitable.

'But how?' I managed to ask.

Hayley explained that Dad had been to the doctor because he'd been having what seemed like really bad bouts of indigestion. The doctor had examined him and found lumps in his neck. Tests had subsequently confirmed non-Hodgkin's lymphoma – a cancer of the lymphatic system.

I tried to take in all the details, but could only consider the implications. 'Is he going to die?' I asked.

After a long pause Hayley replied, 'I don't know.'

I had always been a real daddy's girl. The thought of a life without him was too much to bear. We still had so much of our lives to share. We had plans together. One day I would marry and he would walk me down the aisle. He had spoken of times in the future when he would look after his grandchildren, excited about their staying with him and Mum on our family boat, *Rio Luna*.

Rio Luna had been a big part of my own childhood.

One of the first dates Dad went on with Mum was to see *Breakfast at Tiffany's*, for which the theme tune was 'Moon River'. He used to say, 'One day we'll have a boat and call it *Moon River*.'

Dad had a way of making his dreams come true. He didn't have a qualification to his name, besides O-levels in art and woodwork. But he worked hard, had vision and creativity. He was a true entrepreneur and built up a successful business in Devon. Just as he planned, he bought a boat for the family, and named it *Rio Luna* – Spanish for 'Moon River'. We had so many happy times together on *Rio Luna*. We never crossed oceans but the many days spent bobbing about on the sea in her gave me a confidence that I often drew upon while on *Troika Transatlantic*. The sounds, smells and movements of *Troika* were all similar to those I experienced on *Rio Luna* and often reminded me of the happy times I had spent sharing in Dad's dream.

My childhood memories are full of boat shows, marinas and cruising around the Mediterranean. Dad instilled a love for boats and the ocean in my sister Hayley and me, and from an early age we were complete water babies. Whenever we had the opportunity, we would swim and play in the sea for hours.

Having an identical twin sister is fantastic. She is my best friend, and was with me wherever I went as we grew. We have always been inseparable and were, no doubt, quite a handful for my parents, who also had our two older brothers to look after.

The four children in our family get on brilliantly. It's impossible to tell that Simon, the eldest, and Matthew are Mum and Dad's children by birth and that Hayley and I are adopted. We have always felt privileged to have been drawn into such a loving family and respect Mum and Dad enormously for having the courage to take on another two. Every year they bought us two birthday cakes – the first in July, to celebrate when we were physically born, and another in December, to celebrate the day our adoption papers came through, the day we were 'born' to them.

Dad had worked hard to pay for us to have a good education. Hayley and I were fortunate to attend Stover School, set in acres of beautiful grounds on the edge of Dartmoor. We had taken one look at the big old trees surrounding it and decided it was definitely the school for us! To us avid tree climbers and den makers, it seemed like heaven. We didn't exactly excel at the entrance exams but were already playing tennis for the county and thankfully the head-mistress, Mrs Lunel, saw some potential in us.

My Stover years were very happy years. I excelled at sport, art and music but showed little interest in my academic studies. I developed a love for Dartmoor and hill walking and my sense of adventure flourished through events such as the Ten Tors and the Duke of Edinburgh's Award Scheme. Hayley did well academically and in sport and music. She was confident in her abilities in a way that I was not. In my eyes she had it all and I completely idolised her. I was always one step behind but didn't mind. I thought she was better than I was at everything and wanted everyone else to praise her as I did – and, in general, they would. Hayley became head girl in 1992, while I became head of house – as always, one step behind.

It wasn't until we went our separate ways to different universities at eighteen – Hayley to Lampeter in Wales and I to De Montfort, Bedford – that I realised I had been living my life in Hayley's shadow. At first I couldn't bear to be apart from her. I didn't know how to be one whole person because I had always been half of two. During freshers' week I introduced myself to people by saying, 'Hi, I'm Debra and I have a twin sister called Hayley.' At Bedford, no one knew Hayley, or that I was supposed to be the less intelligent twin. I had held that position for so many years that it had become part of me. It was an unexpected revelation that now, suddenly, I had the freedom to discover just how much I was able to achieve.

Four years on, my degree result did just that. It was a big turning point in my life, and meeting Andrew on that same day seemed significant. Despite my academic success, my time at Bedford had often been unhappy. When Dad became ill in my second year, I began to live life under a foreboding dark cloud. The cloud and I became quite unsociable, so I threw myself into my work. At Henley, the cloud had at last revealed its silver lining.

My first-class results brought with them a rush of confidence that had been missing for some time. Even if all I could do was grin!

It was some weeks before I saw Andrew again. After only a few dates we were very much the love-struck couple, but our lifestyles were quite incompatible. I lived and worked in Devon and he spent his time jetting all over the world, working as a management consultant. Our relationship was characterised by the 'absence makes the heart grow fonder' factor. One week Andrew would be holding meetings in Australia, the next talking to clients in London, while I taught PE at St Margaret's School in Exeter during the week and instructed hill-walking and navigation skills on Dartmoor at the weekends. The time we had together was very precious to us, even if it often involved weekends on Dartmoor with twenty adolescent girls in tow!

It became obvious that Andrew shared my spirit of adventure and love of the outdoors. During my years at Bedford my love for expeditions and sense of adventure had grown. Most weekends and holidays had been filled with mountaineering, rock-climbing and white-water kayaking trips and I had worked at becoming qualified to instructor level in a number of adventure sports. It seemed only natural that at some point Andrew and I should embark on an adventure together.

We saw it as a fantastic opportunity to get to know each other well. There is no hiding the inner depths of your personality when living in extreme conditions. We felt certain that in adventuring we would meet each other's real self in a way that just wouldn't be possible on a two-week package holiday in Europe.

That same year the Challenge Business – for whom my sister Hayley coincidentally worked – had organised and run the first ever Atlantic Rowing Race. It was supposed to be a one-off, but owing to its success the Challenge Business decided to repeat it. Hayley often told us about the race and it immediately appealed to us. The next race was four years ahead, but we felt sure we would still be together – so we entered. With Andrew's rowing background and my expedition experience, we felt certain we had the winning combination. We were so excited by the whole concept and were initially undeterred by the volume of work that would be required just to get the project off the ground. Moreover, it was still four years away. There was plenty of time for the planning and preparations.

We told our parents and friends but I don't think they could really grasp the concept of what we were intending to do. My parents adopted the 'That's nice, dear' attitude. They listened half-heartedly, not fully expecting us to see the project through. They certainly weren't going to lose any sleep over our crazy project just yet.

Around this time, towards the end of 1997, Hayley married Leigh Barnard. I had dreaded Hayley's wedding day as a child, thinking it would signify the day Hayley loved someone more than me! But of course it wasn't at all like that in reality. She was simply moving on to the next stage in her life. We were no longer the twins who shared everything. She had someone else to share her life with now. Despite being happy for Hayley, I felt twinges of sadness about that. But Leigh is such a special person and I could see the happiness he brought to her life.

Andrew and Leigh also began to get to know each other well around this time. They discovered a common link – Ellesmere College in Shropshire. Andrew's parents had taught there and he had attended the school as a pupil between the ages of four and ten. Leigh had worked there years later as a teacher.

When a treasure hunt was organised at the school in July 1998 by a teacher called Sandy Mackinnon, Andrew and Leigh became hooked. Much of that year they chased around the Shropshire countryside looking for clues that would lead them to the elusive silver chalice.

The treasure hunt held a different significance for me. I knew by then that I was to become Mrs Veal. So it seemed vital that Leigh and Andrew develop a strong friendship. If you marry a twin, in some ways you marry the other too – both come very much as a package!

In August of the same year, Andrew and I visited Cornwall. Andrew's family have a special fondness for Cornwall, particularly a stretch of coastal path between Kynance and Mullion. When Andrew was young they holidayed in Cornwall every year, visiting his grandparents, who were born and bred in the county. As children, Andrew and his brother Richard spent hours playing on the south coast beaches and hunting for crabs in the rock pools. Sadly, Andrew's father died of cancer in 1988 and ten years before our visit Andrew had taken his father's ashes to the coastal path to scatter them. So, when Andrew and I followed the path that August day, I was very moved to be visiting that place.

I had never known Andrew's father, so it was the closest I would ever be to him. It also made me think of my own dad's fragility.

It was a sad day – but a happy one, too, for on that beautiful summer's afternoon overlooking a glimmering aquamarine ocean (it seems to pop up everywhere!) Andrew proposed to me.

'What would you say if I told you I have an engagement ring in my pocket?' he taunted.

I told him that I wouldn't believe him. He'd been much too busy to go shopping.

'Wanna bet?' he said.

So I bet Andrew a pint of beer that he hadn't got an engagement ring in his pocket. Then he got down on bended knee and pulled a small blue box from his pocket. As he opened it the bright sunlight glinted off the contents, reflecting splinters of light onto his face. It was the most beautiful sapphire and diamond ring.

I think I still owe him that pint!

Getting engaged to Andrew gave me an enormous sense of completeness. He had become the strong rock in my life. Each of our gifts and abilities complemented those of the other. When I talked about Dad's cancer and he said, 'I understand', I knew he did. He had been through it all with his own father and had come out the other side – something I wasn't confident I could do at that point. Andrew gave me the strength to face what might lie ahead.

Dad was overjoyed at our engagement. He had always had a strong need to provide the best he possibly could for his family. It motivated him throughout his life, driving him to continue to run his business even when he was not well enough to do so. He didn't believe in letting his cancer get in the way of life. I sensed his relief, that, should he die, both Hayley and I had someone special in our lives to partner, care and provide for us. I knew this was important to Dad. In Andrew he saw someone who shared similar beliefs.

By the time we were engaged, Dad had been having courses of chemotherapy for the best part of four years. He always talked about his illness positively – but then he was invariably positive about everything in life. He played it down by never telling me how the treatment was actually going.

I would say, 'But Dad, how is it *really* going?' and he would reply, 'Wonderful, darling – I had smoked salmon for lunch at the hospital, which was rather lovely.' Not your normal run-of-the-mill chemo!

There had been times when Dad was in hospital when things were obviously not going well, but he was adamant that our lives should not change, or that we should be prevented from going away or fulfilling our plans. He hated staying in hospital, so his doctor became brilliant at making allowances for him to go home after his treatment. He even planned the chemotherapy treatment so that Dad could have a week or two off, for a short stay on *Rio Luna*. Maybe he could see how Dad benefited from time on the boat.

My decision to return to Devon to begin teaching had been strongly influenced by a desire to spend as much time as possible with him. The school I taught at was very close to the hospital. But as the year progressed I realised that this was not the best thing for Dad. He didn't have the energy to keep up the positive 'everything's fine' front from day to day. He didn't want any of us to see him suffering, but sometimes it was impossible to hide – especially when I was living with him and Mum. His damaged immune system meant he would get chest infections, which never seemed to clear. I would hear him coughing for hours at night and feel so helpless. I knew he was aware that I was listening to him as he struggled. Both of us became increasingly anxious. So I started to think about moving away and giving Mum and Dad space.

At that time everything seemed to be pointing me towards southwest London. I was engaged to Andrew, who lived there, and had unexpectedly got involved with a new sport on the Thames with my old university friend Charlie – dragon boat racing. The sport involves 22 people – 20 paddlers, a drummer and a steersperson – racing in an elaborately decorated canoe complete with dragon head and tail. Dragon-boat racing requires precise timing and technique combined with raw power.

The muscle groups used for racing dragon boats are similar to those I had developed through kayaking, so I picked it up quickly. After only a few months I found myself at the Great Britain time trials and set one of the fastest times. Once I had secured a place in the GB squad for the European Championships, the long drive from Devon to Kingston for training sessions was impractical, so I looked for a new teaching job near southwest London.

The coach of the GB squad, Griff, believed in focusing on the mental training – using the power of the mind – as much as physical training. At first I struggled and didn't feel it made any difference to my physical performance. But Griff's continued encouragement and endless 'just imagine' work sheets began to take effect. 'Visualisation' and 'mental rehearsal' became part of my everyday language. He taught me powerful lessons that became vital during my time on *Troika Transatlantic*.

In September 1998 Mum, Dad and Andrew travelled to Rome to watch me race in the European Championships. I had always wanted to represent my country in a sport, so it was a dream come true. Walking out in my Great Britain kit meant the world to me, and just as much to Mum and Dad. When I went up to collect my bronze and silver medals at the end of the championships, Dad was tearful with pride. I hadn't seen Mum and Dad looking so happy for ages. Dad's hair had just grown back after another course of chemotherapy and he looked really well. I took a photo of Mum, Dad and Charlie's mum, Barbara, just before I went up to collect my medals. The smiles on their faces said it all, and the pride in Dad's eyes that day is something I'll never forget. Three years later, I carried that photo to sea with me to remind myself how happy it made him to see me fulfilling my dreams.

I began a new job at Claremont Fan Court School in Esher, Surrey, in September 1998, arriving a little after term had begun because of an overlap with the European Championships. I had been sad to leave St Margaret's School in Exeter but departed with a new furry friend, who would later join us in our row across the Atlantic. Charlotte Wood, a pupil from the junior school, had given me a teddy bear as a leaving present. I named him 'Woody' after her surname. He became a vital member of the *Troika* crew. No boat is complete without a ship's bear!

Despite the challenge of a new job, and a need to start focusing on the Atlantic rowing race, I couldn't wait to begin training for the Dragon Boat World Championships. They were planned for

September 1999, just a few months after our wedding, the special day I had always dreamed of, when Dad would have a very significant part to play.

Dad always talked about events in the future as if cancer would never prevent him from being part of them. I wanted Dad's future to extend way beyond that special day, so the World Championships were my way of giving him something to focus on beyond the wedding. I also wanted to see that pride in his eyes again.

In December that year, Dad announced that he wanted to take the whole family to Austria for Christmas. This was something we had done when Hayley and I were eleven years old and it had been one of the best family times we had ever had. We stayed in the beautiful resort of Zell am Zee. Every day Andrew and I skied with my brothers, and Hayley and Leigh. We were all at quite different standards but it didn't matter. We were just having the best time together, laughing nonstop – probably because we were spending a bit too long resting in the mountain cafés, drinking round after round of hot mulled wine!

I would rush back to shower at the end of every afternoon, before heading for the pre-dinner drinks in Mum and Dad's hotel room. Dad was always full of the party spirit in the evening and would entertain us all, getting the evening off to a swinging start. He'd always known how to throw a good party. This was the highlight of my day. I could not have been happier than when we were sitting around together, joking about a spectacular 'head plant' into the snow that one of us had done, or some such frivolous event. The feeling of family unity and togetherness was very special.

But, on a few of the days I visited his room early in the afternoon, I found him in bed looking very unwell. He often had to rest all day just to have enough energy to cope with the family times in the evenings. Mum would go out for long walks, leaving him to sleep.

He really was not well, but generally disguised it successfully. He was as outwardly positive as ever but looked tired and coughed continually. I began to worry about his motives for the trip and couldn't help wondering if he wanted the family to be together one last time before he died. Perhaps he sensed that his body could not take much more of the treatment. Perhaps he and Mum both knew something we didn't, or recognised that time was short. I was too scared to ask, and kept my concerns to myself. We were having such a wonderful family time that it didn't seem right to ask.

By New Year I had almost convinced myself that I was wrong, and that Dad was fine. The day before New Year's Eve Hayley and I were agents in the final mission to dig up the treasure that Andrew and Leigh had been hunting for a whole year! It was just the distraction I needed. Andrew and Leigh, now firm friends, were like two excited children. They had known for some weeks that the silver chalice was buried by a monument near Llangollen and had been waiting for an opportunity to drive to North Wales to claim their prize.

Digging up the treasure together sealed what had become a special friendship, for Andrew had already asked Leigh to be his best man at our wedding. Hayley and I were overjoyed, not only by the way things had turned out between our respective 'other halves', but because we no longer had to spend weekends walking around the churchyards and monuments of Shropshire looking for clues to buried treasure! Finding the treasure was a great start to 1999. Surely, we thought, this was a good omen. We had our wedding to look forward to in July, World Championship medals to win in September and the Ward Evans Atlantic Rowing Challenge to plan. It was an exciting and busy time and we were full of optimism.

The months before the wedding were inevitably hectic as I was also training for the Great Britain Dragon Boat time-trial weekend. I desperately wanted to make the squad, but knew the time I would spend 'out' for the wedding and honeymoon would be against me. Mum and Dad were brilliant at working with me to organise the wedding and I was particularly pleased that Dad was so involved. I didn't have many free weekends because of my training commitments, but I returned to Devon whenever I could to join in the excitement and the plans with both of them.

In June we returned to Rose Cottage, the family home, for a final planning weekend and my wedding-dress fitting. Hayley and Leigh joined us, so Dad decided to arrange one of his famous barbecues. The wine and beer flowed as freely as it always did when Dad was entertaining – but unfortunately the rain flowed, too! We ended up crammed into the garden shed with our food and laughed away at anything and everything. I left them all at the end of that weekend, hardly able to wait for us all to be together again for our wedding, and thinking how lucky I was to have such a special family.

It was the last time I saw Dad alive.

A few days later I arrived at school early and headed for the staff room and a chat with one of my colleagues, Sam. I told her something Dad had said at the weekend that had stuck in my mind: 'If anything happens to me in the future you mustn't change your plans.' He had merely slipped it into our conversation without dwelling on the point. I told Sam that I took it to mean that if he should die before the wedding we should go ahead with it, as planned. He was always telling me that I should do whatever I wanted to do in life and let nothing stand in my way, so I couldn't be one hundred per cent sure that he was talking about the wedding. But there was something about the way he said it. He hadn't looked unwell, but by then he was an expert at being the positive, happy dad who didn't have a worry in the world. I could never have known how ill he was.

As I walked out of the staff room and through the entrance hall I saw Andrew running up the steps towards me. His face was expressionless and he didn't return my smile of surprise at seeing him at school. He stopped inches in front of me.

'It's your dad.'

That's all he had to say. I knew the rest.

My world felt as if it had ended with those three short words, although I had been expecting them for years. Every time the phone rang I would immediately think: is this the phone call telling me that Dad has gone? Much as I had prepared myself for it, imagined it, or thought I had come to terms with the expectation, nothing could have prepared me for that moment. I knew for the first time what it meant to be heartbroken. It had just been a figure of speech before, but now I knew it as a physical as well as an emotional pain. The ache remained in my heart for months.

'Why now?' I asked Andrew. 'Why couldn't he have waited just a few more weeks? After all this time, I thought he was going to make it – he was going to walk me down the aisle.'

I wasn't aware that I was shouting, of the pupils flooding past me into school, or my hysterical behaviour. I was trapped in a private painful world where nothing but injustice and cruelty seemed to make sense. All my life I had dreamed of the moment when Dad would walk me down the aisle and now it wouldn't happen.

He had so narrowly missed our moment.

The day of Dad's funeral was painfully ironic. I walked down the aisle – but behind Dad's coffin. The friends and family members I passed would be returning to the same church just in a few weeks' time for my wedding. The florist who was planning our wedding flowers had made a perfect three-dimensional model of *Rio Luna* out of flowers. I focused on it with all my might as the service ran its course, remembering the happy days that we had spent on the boat together as a family.

Outside I held Mum's and Hayley's hands as we watched Dad's coffin being lowered into the grave. I held some petals I had picked from the roses that climbed the front of the cottage, and waited to scatter them there. Dad had been so happy living in Rose Cottage and I wanted a small bit of it to be with him. The three of us all held something we wanted to leave there. Mum put in a photo of *Rio Luna* and Hayley had written Dad a letter.

I kept looking down at the coffin and at the brass plaque engraved with Dad's name to check that it was definitely his. Eventually Hayley pulled me away.

It just didn't seem real. It was a beautiful day, the birds were singing and the sun was shining. It wasn't a day to be sad. I couldn't help thinking that it was Dad's doing. He used to tell us not to be sad when he died but to have a big party, give everyone a drink and celebrate his life. He was content with everything he had achieved. It was a level of contentment that I would aspire to myself.

The weeks before the wedding were emotional but I knew what Dad wanted me to do. I tried to hold everything together, but there were times when the stress of organising, and the tactlessness of a few, made me want to postpone it. Andrew was the most amazing support. He instinctively seemed to know when to speak, when to give me space, or when just to hold me as I cried.

The night before the wedding I couldn't sleep at all. I was concerned about how the day would go. I just didn't know what to expect. I was worried that Mum would have to face such a big day alone and wondered what the mood of the day would be under the circumstances.

Bubbling under the surface of my worries was a genuine excite-ment about starting married life with Andrew. As I lay thinking through the night hours, my thoughts flew ahead two years to the start line of the Atlantic Rowing Challenge. I had seen the film footage of the start of the 1997 race so was able to picture the scene quite clearly in my mind.

I imagined us sitting on our little rowing boat at the start, excited about beginning our big adventure together. I could almost feel the warmth of the sun on my skin and smell the ocean. Despite my sadness, there was so much to look forward to.

I watched Hayley sleeping next to me in the room we had always shared. She looked so peaceful. My thoughts returned to the day ahead – I thought of Dad and was filled with the most wonderful feeling of joy. It almost took me by surprise. I felt as if Dad were with me and knew everything was going to be fine.

That joy lasted throughout the day and was shared among the guests. But I still worried for Mum. It was hard for her to face the day without Dad by her side. My brothers were brilliant. Simon walked me down the aisle and Matthew gave the father-of-the-bride speech at the reception at Stover School. It was a perfect day with the sun shining and the champagne flowing. Inscribed in Latin on our wedding cake were the words 'In Love, Friendship and Adventures Everlasting'. They seemed to sum up our relationship perfectly.

It was wonderful to be back in the glorious surroundings of Stover for our wedding day. The trees were as big and beautiful as ever and I could not resist climbing my favourite tree to celebrate the day. It was quite a challenge in the masses of white fabric that made up the skirt of my wedding dress, but worth the effort, and captured beautifully by our artistic photographer.

True to the inscription on our wedding cake, we wanted our adventure together to begin from day one of our married life. Leaving the reception by hot-air balloon was the perfect start. We rose up from the lacrosse fields where I had spent so many hours competing as a youngster, to be presented with the most spectacular view of Dartmoor. Beneath us lay the Tors, rocks and curved valleys where my adventures had begun as a child. It was a delight to experience them from such a stunning vantage point on our special day. As we gently floated higher we were embraced by the silence. I wondered if we would experience similar moments of tranquillity in the middle of the Atlantic.

We looked down on all our guests, each one becoming ant-like in appearance as we ascended. If Dad had been down there, standing next to Mum, he would have been looking skywards and probably would have been heard saying, 'How marvellous.'

Chapter 3

Getting to the Start Line

The eight-hour flight to Africa, our honeymoon destination, was the first opportunity I had to stop and think about what had happened over the previous two months. The lead-up to the wedding had been so busy and, with the event now over, it began to sink in that Dad really wasn't coming back. It was supposed to be a special time for Andrew and me – and it was – but I increasingly found that memories of my time with Dad consumed my thoughts. Although I had Andrew to share the future with, I couldn't stop thinking that for Dad and me together there was no future – at least this side of heaven.

Travel, for me, has always brought on periods of reflection. Distance from everything that's familiar encourages it. We are given a chance to see our own small world from the vantage point of another, and camping on the banks of the Zambezi could not have been a more perfect place for it.

Many afternoons were spent sipping cold beers with Andrew and discussing what the future could hold. What I needed was a mental challenge to fill some of the emptiness left by Dad's death. Physically I had all the bases covered – both the Dragon Boat Racing World Championships and the Atlantic Rowing Race to look forward to – but mentally I did not feel stimulated in my job.

I had discussed the idea of starting an Internet company with two friends. So, many drinks later, when Andrew's management consultant's brain had been well and truly picked, a business model was drawn. A decision had been made. It was time for me to follow in Dad's footsteps and have a go at being an entrepreneur. Little did I know at the time just how demanding life was about to become. The gap Dad had left may have been starting to fill, but the underlying issues had not been touched.

Starting a business, while teaching full-time, training for World Championships and getting used to my new role as a wife was more than a little stressful! I had taken on too much and, being a perfectionist, tried to commit totally to everything. Andrew had also started a new job and was fully engrossed. There wasn't any time to start preparing to row the Atlantic!

The Dragon Boat World Championships were a cause of much personal disappointment and heartache. Mum, Andrew and Simon were there to watch, but it just wasn't the same without Dad. I did not perform to the best of my ability and had lost much of my focus. I had gone from being one of the fastest in the crew at the European Championships to sitting on the bench for certain races at the Worlds. I was angry and disappointed with myself, as I knew I was capable of so much more.

On return I threw myself into the creation of what had become The Well Hung Art Company – an online art gallery and consultancy. The business really began to take shape and I knew I couldn't maintain another full-time job alongside my role as managing director for long. So in the summer of 2000 I took a leap of faith, supported by Andrew, and gave up my teaching career to focus on the company.

Andrew was amazingly encouraging but let me make my own mistakes. As a management consultant he had spent years advising companies how to run their businesses better. He saw what would and would not have worked with Well Hung Art so often, but stayed quiet, preferring to let me discover the way for myself. He was always there for me, but gave advice only when I specifically asked for his help. Consequently, my business confidence grew.

Our respective 'business' roles, to a certain extent, reflected those we had adopted in our marriage. Perhaps that was why it was such a shock to both of us when our roles were reversed during our first two weeks at sea. Until then, Andrew always seemed to have the answers. My job was mainly to encourage him and help him through the hard times. At sea he suddenly needed me to be the one to find the answers and give advice. It felt good to be the rock in our relationship for the first time, to reciprocate all that he had been for me in the previous few years.

I didn't think any less of him because I had to provide the mental and emotional support, and Andrew didn't struggle with accepting my help. His ability to accept that he needed support is itself evidence of strength of character, but it is often overlooked. We had always believed that rowing the Atlantic as a husband-and-wife team would be a real advantage. It was a great opportunity for us to learn and grow in our marriage as partners.

We would never have predicted the way things turned out, and nor would our friends and acquaintances. They believed it was I who would struggle at sea, and often made comments to Andrew, suggesting that, if he was really serious about winning the race, he should go with another man. We were both amazed by the response we had when we told people we were entering the race together. The offhand comments and stunned looks we received said it all, especially when we talked to other rowers. We had no idea that we still lived in such a sexist world.

A conversation we had at Henley Royal Regatta in July 2000 was a prime illustration of this pervading attitude. Andrew, Joanna and I met an old rowing acquaintance in the Farley Bar. The conversation turned to the Atlantic Rowing Race.

'Who are you rowing with?' asked the six-foot-five acquaintance, himself a rower.

'My wife,' Andrew replied, looking Mr Six-Foot-Five straight in the eyes at matching height. Six-Foot-Five immediately turned to Joanna, who is a six-foot, lean 'rowing goddess' of a woman, assumed she was Andrew's wife and started asking her about the race. I was ignored. The conversation was all taking place way above my five-foot-five-high head, anyway, and I began to feel like a very little girl. I expected pigtails to sprout from the sides of my head and a lollipop to suck at any minute!

'Jo's not my wife,' Andrew said, relieving an embarrassed Joanna. '*This* is my wife.'

He gestured proudly downwards to my less significant stature. The look on Six-Foot-Five's face was a picture: it was a mixture of utter disbelief and brazen disgust. After what seemed like an eternity, he finally gestured towards Joanna and said, 'Well, mate, if you're going to row the Atlantic with a woman you should at least go with one this size!'

I can laugh now, but at the time I was getting pretty sick of it. Enduring reactions that suggested that I was not big enough, strong enough or in any way the right person to partner Andrew in the race began to play on my self-confidence. I decided the only action I could take would be to burn all the negative comments and convert them into fuel for my own determination. I would prove the sceptics wrong – and how!

The only exceptions to my rule came in honest discussion with close friends such as Joanna and Pete King. They had become our best friends. We had met on the same night, on the same 'party boat' at Henley. Joanna Biggin became Joanna King when they married just a few months after us, and our lives have continued to draw endless parallels ever since. Pete and Andrew had rowed together, and both Joanna and Pete knew us well. They became the key players in our support crew. One night we were having dinner with Joanna and Pete and discussed the planned race, as we so often did. I made some comment about winning and Pete replied, 'You don't really think you could *win*, do you?'

I was absolutely flabbergasted. 'Why *shouldn't* I think we could win?' I replied.

Joanna looked worried, as she sensed immediately that Pete had said the worst thing he could about my hopes for the race.

'Well,' he said tentatively, 'you surely can't expect to go faster than a crew that contains two big strong guys.'

Pete was one of the few people who I thought understood the strength of our team. I'd always believed he had faith in my ability. He even knew the facts: that a husband-and-wife team had come third in the 1997 race and that even other male–female teams of rowers had done well. Pete is very knowledgeable about sports psychology, and knows only too well the power of the mind when it comes to sports performance. Yet he did what everyone else had done. He took my physical size to mean that I could not compete with the men's teams. I was deeply hurt.

It's true that if you put me side by side with a guy on a rowing ergometer, I could not possibly compete over a short distance: my limb length alone would prevent me from pulling as effectively. But that is not what this particular race is about. It is a race over three thousand miles where anything and everything can happen, and more than physical strength is required to win.

I felt drained after Pete's comments and desperately tried to hide how upset I was. If my own support team didn't believe I could win, then no one else would. I knew that Pete had not meant anything personally and that he would have been sad if he had known how deeply I had felt his comments. I love Pete dearly. He is one of my best friends, so I felt awful when he later apologised. I obviously hadn't hidden my feelings well enough.

That conversation had quite an impact on my confidence. I started to wonder if maybe Andrew felt the same as Pete, and whether deep down he was disappointed to be going with me; that he, too, thought we would not be able to win because of my size. I shared my concerns with Andrew and he soon put me straight. 'I wouldn't want to go with anyone other than you,' he said. 'We're the perfect team.'

Subject closed!

With a year to go we had done very little towards getting prepared for the race other than paying the entry fee by monthly direct debit. We would turn up at the Challenge Business race briefings and have nothing prepared. Other crews had studied the race rules, found sponsors and even proudly shown photos of their baby boats. It was obvious that, for some of the crews, rowing the Atlantic was a main focus, consuming the whole of their day-to-day lives. They had known few distractions or life-changing events. It just wasn't the same for us, so we weren't worried. We had started a business, been competing internationally in our respective sports, had got married, bought a house and lost a parent. We just hadn't had time to focus on a race that, until that point, had been years away.

Even if we had built our boat, we wouldn't have had anywhere to keep it and storage space isn't cheap in London. So with a year to go we pulled together a support crew and started to brainstorm, working out what needed to be done. For me it was obvious – I had to learn how to row!

I had been socialising with rowers for years but had always managed to avoid getting in a boat, preferring to run along the bank with the water bottles and a bunch of bananas. I didn't have the faintest idea how to row. Although I had been involved with water sports such as kayaking and dragon boating for some years, they are completely different from rowing and few of my skills could be transferred. For starters, you don't even face the same way! It took me quite some time to get used to doing a sport backwards. I also had to develop my leg strength, as my previous water sports were far more upper-body-oriented.

A week's course in the summer of 2000 at Tideway Scullers School soon sorted that out. I immediately loved it, and became determined to be the best I could be in the shortest time possible. I was on the river at six o'clock most mornings, spellbound by the feeling of gliding along the surface of the water. As the winter drew near, the cold, crisp, still mornings were beautiful. I would slide through the early-morning mist that rose from the water with the sun emerging above me.

Rowing with Andrew was quite a different experience. As we took to a double scull with the aim of learning how to respond to each other in a small boat, I found plenty to respond to! I had never really witnessed Andrew in a competitive situation or one in which he was pushing himself, so was quite surprised at what I discovered. His mood often darkened in the boat and he motivated himself by getting angry and shouting at himself. This was the complete opposite to me and – in normal life – to him. Andrew is always on the same happy and emotionally steady level, so I was somewhat shocked. It was hard not to assume that, as I was the only other person in the boat, I must be the one who was causing this change in mood. It took some getting used to. We had been right: this certainly was providing us with plenty of opportunities to discover the depths of each other's personality – and we had hardly started yet!

In a token bid to get our Atlantic rowing campaign going, we headed for the start location, Los Gigantes in Tenerife, a year to the day before we were due to set off. We convinced ourselves that it was more than a holiday: a 'recce' was an important part of our race preparations! It *was* a very useful trip. We observed the weather conditions and sea state, found accommodation, met some of the locals and located the ship's chandlers and supermarkets. Having that familiarity gave us confidence in what to expect when we would pitch up in Tenerife a year later. Most importantly, we became very enthusiastic about the race, and returned to England fully charged to begin the hard work.

We had been told by a number of competitors from the 1997 race that getting to the start line was the hardest part and, without a doubt, it was. The race organisers, the Challenge Business, had set a 50-boat limit on the race. The places were soon filled and a long waiting list developed, but the nearer the teams got to having to pay their final entry money, the more teams dropped out. Planning to row the Atlantic is financially crippling, so obtaining sponsorship money was a top priority. Getting the boat and equipment was also a priority, but we could not do one without the other.

Finding sponsorship was an endless, thankless task. Ocean rowing is not a recognised sport and therefore unpredictable as an event to sponsor. There was also the issue of success rates. Before the first race in 1997, more people had been to the moon than had successfully rowed across the Atlantic and just under half of those who had tried had not made it. We tried to get round this by offering companies the chance to put their logo underneath on the hull where, should we capsize, brand exposure would be guaranteed, but they remained unconvinced!

The year 2001 progressed at speed and the opportunity arose to lease a fully built Atlantic rowing boat. It was brand-new. The owners were unable to participate in the race, as one half of the team had not been granted the time off from his pilot training in the RAF. Normally the boats arrive as 34 sheets of plywood in a box, so not having to build the shell at that late stage, especially without funding, was handy, to say the least.

The boat arrived in March, leaving us just six months to turn it into an ocean-going vessel. The bills from the boat builders and equipment suppliers seemed endless, so, when Andrew found himself without a job, our situation did not look good. But someone was on our side. Andrew discovered that his skills and experience were in demand and, by boldly negotiating sponsorship and three months off as part of his job package, we were able unexpectedly to gain a sponsor! For larger consultancies the sponsorship money would have been nothing, but it had been a small company, Troika, that caught Andrew's eye. Their amazing work–life balance attitude was irresistible. They were not in a position to throw huge sums of money at the sponsorship but said they would do what they could. So *Troika Transatlantic* was born and Andrew had a new job.

The boat preparation progressed slowly. We had found a sponsor and the physical training was well under way. It was time to fill the gaps in our knowledge. Weekends – both of us already exhausted from our full-time jobs, boat building and midweek training – were spent in the classroom. Ocean navigation and metrology, VHF radio, sea survival and a host of other courses were completed. Then we had to learn how to fix equipment such as the water maker. That piece of kit was to be our lifeline – no purified water, no race – so we had to be able to fix it should it go wrong.

The months slipped by and still the boat was nowhere near

completion. The boatyard in Windsor whose services we used took on too many rowing boats and there just wasn't enough time to get them all completed. With just a few months to go, we started heading to the yard after work in the vain attempt to assist the boat builder, working late into the night and often into the early hours of the morning. It was only the fixtures and fittings that needed attention, but the list seemed endless and each small job took hours.

The stress of preparations meant we began to lose sight of the goal – to row across the Atlantic. We could see only as far ahead as the end of the next problem with *Troika Transatlantic*. Other teams felt much the same. Some had not even built the shell of their boat, owing to lack of funding. We really felt for these crews and others who were falling by the wayside.

In many ways the stress was great preparation for life at sea. We had a dry run of being under pressure and trying not to take it out on each other! We were working closely as a team, setting goals and overcoming obstacles, and we were getting there slowly with the help of our fantastic support crew – Joanna and Pete King, my wonderful twin Hayley and her husband Leigh. Pete, also a management consultant, ran our planning meetings with military precision. Each of us was given a list of tasks and deadlines, all leading to the big day – 11 September – when *Troika Transatlantic* would be taken to Felixstowe and put on a container ship to the Canary Islands. It was to become a much more significant day than we had expected. A day that changed the world, for ever.

With *Troika Transatlantic* in a reasonable state, we began a series of weekend sea trials. Joanna and Pete gave of their time freely to help with these and made life significantly easier for us. But almost every sea trial was scuppered by strong winds – often blowing in completely the wrong direction. We were either washed onto the rocks off the Welsh coast or pushed out to sea off the south coast of England. When we did finally manage to row *Troika* into the shelter of Poole Harbour, she was rammed by a 63-foot motor cruiser, which ripped off a side panel and bent the riggers. This was not part of Pete's meticulous plan!

Some good did come out of the sea trials. As we finally pushed away from Fishguard on the Welsh coast and shouted to Joanna and Pete, 'See you on Monday,' it suddenly hit me – three days alone at sea with Andrew. I could see that Andrew felt it too and was as excited as I was. There had been so much talk. Everyone had been asking us about the race and we had been constantly sharing the dream. It felt fantastic to be finally living it, if only for a few days. There was certainly no indication that Andrew's enthusiasm would later turn to fear.

Life on board was new and thrilling. Everything was a learning curve. It wasn't so much the rowing – we knew how to do that – but the day-to-day living on board a small boat that was fascinating: how best to cook, clean and go to the loo in a swell; where to sit or stand when Andrew was rowing so that I was not in the way or unbalancing the boat; which bit of our food parcels I could digest at which times of the day and how to respond to Andrew's 'changing moods'. All these things had to be worked at, and I loved the challenge they presented.

Owing to the vast amount of energy we used during our twelve hours of rowing a day, we had calculated that it was necessary to consume 8,000 calories for every 24-hour period.

At four times the normal recommended daily allowance, this might seem like bliss to a chocoholic, but it was a horrendous amount to get through in a day. As well as specialist expedition food, we carried a vast range of snack foods and other meals.

To ensure that we would consume enough calories each day, Joanna, Pete, Andrew and I spent four days packing a carefully chosen variety into day packs. Andrew and I had a daily pack each, which in theory should have been empty by the end of each 24-hour period. It rarely was. Even on our training weekends, we seldom ate more than a third.

Example of a 'day pack' menu

Breakfast	Foil-packed bacon and beans, hot chocolate and Frosties cereal bar, pitta bread and jam.
Mid-morning snack	SIS Go (power) bar, tea/coffee.
Lunch	Pasta and sauce, foil-packed pudding (e.g. spotted dick).
Mid-afternoon snack	Mixed fruits and nuts, cereal bar.
Evening meal	Crisps, foil-packed meal (e.g. beef stew and dumplings), foil-packed chocolate pudding and chocolate sauce, hot drink.
Late-evening snack	Noodles, Cup-a-Soup, chocolate bar.
Night-time snack	Hot chocolate, shortbread, Jaffa cakes, Go (power) bar.
Extra shared snacks	Biscuits, dried apricots, mangoes and prunes.
Liquid consumption	5 litres of Science In Sport PSP22 carbohydrate energy, fuel-solution drink and 3 litres of water.

After an all-nighter at the boatyard on 10 September *Troika Transatlantic* was still not finished. But we had run out of time. My friend and business partner, Andrew 'Ferg' Fergusson, had arranged to tow the boat to Felixstowe, from where it was to be shipped to Spain. We broke down three times on the way, continuing the tradition that nothing with *Troika Transatlantic* was ever going to be easy. But our stressful day paled into insignificance when we received a phone call from Ferg's girlfriend informing us that two planes had crashed into the side of the Twin Towers in New York.

The radio confirmed the worst. We drove back sombrely, listening to the news reports. It certainly put things into perspective for us.

There was a strange calm before the storm after the boat had gone. There was nothing we could do about it until we got to Tenerife, so the focus switched to sorting out our lives in preparation for being out of contact with our family, friends, and work for at least two months. Joanna and Pete, who lived only two miles away, were given our bank details and keys to the house and were generally put in charge of our lives. It takes a special kind of friendship to be able to trust people to that level, and special they certainly are.

My biggest task was completing the handover of my role as managing director of The Well Hung Art Company to Lizzie Baird, who was left holding the baby in my absence. The transfer had been operating for some months, but, inevitably, the last week before the final handover was stressful. I had spent the best part of two years building the company from scratch and had taken little time off because of the necessary hard work required to foster a fledgling company. Leaving it for an unknown number of months was a real wrench for me.

After *Troika* had left for Tenerife ahead of us, we tried to fit in as many visits as possible to friends and family. We had been working so hard on the boat for the previous three months that we had spent little time with any of them. I always wondered, as we said our goodbyes, whether we would see them again. Not in any melo-dramatic way, but purely because there is no controlling the elements and I knew that anything could happen. In my diary on the plane to Tenerife on Friday 21 September I wrote:

```
As I sit here checking my notes on
Tropical Revolving Storms (hurricanes)
I'm finding it hard to suppress my
excitement. I'm listening to 'Chilled
Ibiza' on my MP3 Jukebox, bopping in my
seat as everyone around me tries to
```

```
sleep. I can't believe this day is
finally here. I'm ready.
```

The previous two months had been incredibly busy. We were mentally, physically and emotionally drained. I could never have imagined that getting to the start line would be so hard. We were almost at breaking point when, a few days before the flight, we were sent a bill for over £24,000 from the boat builder. It was thousands more than we had estimated. We couldn't imagine where we were expected to get that kind of money when we were just about to leave the country for two or more months. At a special leaving drinks party the Troika company directors called us aside to tell us that they were so proud of what we were achieving that they didn't want us to be worrying about money before we'd even started. They promised to lend us what we needed. With that kind of support, we thought, how could we fail?

I had aimed to take time out once we arrived in Tenerife, to spend some time looking out to sea and being still. I wanted to focus, practise my visualisation techniques and mentally rehearse so that psychologically I was prepared and in the right mindset for the weeks ahead. No such luck.

We and some of the other teams were expecting the boat builder from England, who was going to fly to Tenerife to complete outstanding work on the vessels. Unfortunately, because of his workload, the boat builder turned up a week late, by which time we had taken it upon ourselves to complete the work and not rely on anyone else. This was one of the best decisions we made regarding the boat. It opened doors and introduced us to many of the other 34 teams of competitors from 13 different countries. Every boat had something that needed finishing and a few were only half built! The camaraderie between the teams grew stronger every day as competitors borrowed each other's tools and tubes of Sikkaflex.

Not all the teams were so friendly, though. As the only mixed team in the race, we were not perceived to be a threat to the 'big-boy' teams and a few of the competitors did not even bother giving me the time of day. The arrogance of some crews was startling – but then I suppose it was a testosterone-filled race!

I discussed this with Simon Walpole, one day on the way to the ship's chandler. Simon was a competitor from Guernsey, racing in a boat named *UniS Voyager*. Physically, Simon did not look a patch on the six-foot-plus strapping rowers. He is not particularly tall and has a slight frame. But he also has a wiry endurance, and to judge him by his appearance alone is deceiving. He felt that some of the competitors regarded him in a similar light to the way they regarded me. We spoke honestly for some time before Simon finally admitted, 'Debra, the reason the other competitors don't take you seriously is because you don't look butch enough to be a threat. Frankly, you're just too pretty and girlie.' I appreciated Simon's honesty and knew deep down that he was probably right. Perhaps I had even played up to that image because I just didn't see why I should try to be anything else. Surely, I thought, you can still be feminine and row the Atlantic! It wasn't just the men, though. One young woman asked me if I would be rowing or was going along to do the cooking and cleaning!

We finally got the boat in the water four days before the start and rowed out to sea, mainly to test the water maker. When Andrew went to open the inlet valve, it came off in his hand, producing a small fountain effect in the middle of the boat.

'Turn around and start rowing back to the harbour!' said Andrew. 'Quick!'

The urgency in his voice got me moving the oars through the water as fast as I could. Water flooded in through the hole in the bottom of the boat, while Andrew attempted to stop the flow with his thumb.

'We'd better add some corks to the shopping list,' I said.

My ill-timed joke was not well received!

It wasn't the first challenge of the race and it certainly wouldn't be the last.

Sure enough, the following day the next problem presented itself. We had intended to take a laptop, which we would connect to the satellite phone so that we could send emails. I had planned to keep in touch with the other directors of The Well Hung Art Company in this way. We had also planned to send email diary updates back to the support team for friends, family and sponsors, and to update our team website. But in an attempt to get the laptop to speak to the satellite phone we discovered that they were incompatible. As we tried to fix the problem, the laptop fatally crashed.

The only option was to use the satellite phone alone and read out any emails and updates down the phone for the support team to forward. It was another cloud that turned out to have a silver lining because it gave me an excuse to talk to the support team more often (despite the phone bill!) and I was forced to abandon all ideas of continuing my role as managing director while at sea: no laptop – no emails – no work!

The night before the start our friends and family congregated on our balcony with bottles of champagne. For some reason I couldn't face it. I busied myself packing our bags and made it look as though I were tying up loose ends. I didn't want to offend anyone, so stayed out of the way until it was time for us all to go to the restaurant for our 'last-night' meal.

The atmosphere over dinner was relaxed and playful, but I could feel little of it. I munched my way through every vegetable on the table, making the most of the last opportunity for fresh food. Pete gave a hilarious demonstration of how to kill and fillet a fish, using his rolled-up napkin to mimic the fish. I knew I was going to miss Sunday night curries with Joanna and Pete.

As we stood outside the apartment blocks it was suddenly time to say our goodbyes to Mum and my brothers. Andrew and I had to be on board *Troika* early the next morning, and due to transport problems between Los Gigantes, where we were all staying, and Playa San Juan, where *Troika* was berthed, we knew we were unlikely to have time for goodbyes in the morning. Mum hugged me and said, 'Bye, darling. Take care, and I'll see you in Barbados.' I didn't expect her to say any more than that. After all, what do you say to your daughter when she is about to row 3,000 miles across an ocean? Mum believed in me and was sure I could do it. The boys were cheerful too, but I knew that Matthew would want to say more. We had previously talked about how our family is sometimes slow to express its love in words (but not in actions) and I knew Matt wanted that to change.

With the goodbyes over, I still felt nothing – neither happiness nor sadness, nervousness nor calm. I just felt blank. I couldn't understand it. And yet, if anything went wrong, I knew I might never see my family again. Looking back, I realise that just reaching the start line had left me exhausted and emotionally drained. It was time to get going.

Sleep did not come easily that night. It's common enough – you have to get up early for something so you spend the night checking the clock to see if you have overslept, or how much longer you can sleep. It was the same for me that night. I gave up at 5 a.m. and took a shower, savouring it as my last for some time. Little did I know just how long it would be before the next one.

As I sat on the balcony watching the dawn break, I remembered the good-luck cards I had brought for all the other teams. I hadn't had a chance to write them and had now run out of time. I was annoyed with myself, as it was something I had felt very strongly about doing. Whether they made it across the pond or not, I knew how hard it had been for each member of every crew to get to that day. Whether they came in first or last, they were all about to achieve something extraordinary.

As Joanna, Pete, Hayley and Leigh arrived, I felt incredibly calm and lacking in emotion. Joanna's bottom lip was already trembling and she had one major crying fit before we even left the balcony. My family were quite used to my going off to do crazy things, but Joanna wasn't. My lack of emotion didn't mean I didn't care, but made me feel a little awkward. Andrew looked similarly relaxed. But, then, he usually does.

When we arrived at Playa San Juan, where the rowing boats were moored, I was surprised how few competitors had arrived. Still numb, I stood with Joanna, who was still crying. Crews drifted in slowly with a distinct lack of urgency.

With the final goodbyes over, I jumped into a tender waiting to take me out to *Troika Transatlantic*, where Andrew was waiting for me, making the last-minute checks. As we wove in and out of the fishing boats, I spotted *New Zealand Telecom Challenge 25*. They were the only all female crew and the only other women in the race out of 70 competitors. I had genuine respect for them both.

I shouted across to them, 'Steph! Jude! See you in Barbados!' They shouted and waved back, looking every bit the part – tall, strong, athletic and well disciplined. I knew they would do well. I'd said, 'See you in Barbados' to a number of crews, but the chances of really doing so were slim. I felt certain that we would be in the top ten, maybe even the top five, and would therefore be gone before the crews at the back of the fleet arrived. Ironically, I vowed that I would make the effort to be on the quayside to 'see in' every crew to arrive in Barbados while we were still there.

In a moment, Andrew and I were in *Troika Transatlantic* and ready to go. That moment had been a long time coming. I sat on my rowing seat looking at Andrew, who stood in the foot well looking at me. 'Well, here we are, then,' he said, as we grinned at each other. We were like two excited children on Christmas morning, not because of any adrenaline-pumping anticipation of racing the other competitors, but because we had finally made it to the start day.

We were also exhausted and wanted to get out to sea for a rest! But we intended to make the most of every minute of the adventure and live it to the max. Most of all, I was looking forward to spending 24 hours a day with Andrew. As I looked at him, I was overwhelmed by my feelings for him. He was radiant.

The weather was glorious as we rowed out of the harbour. We moved away from the other boats for a while, wanting some time to compose our minds and stretch. The sun was bright, reflecting off the surface of the water, making it appear crystal clear. There were no ripples, just big rolling swells caused by a stiff breeze. The atmosphere as we rowed back towards the others was electric. Tim and Jonathan (a.k.a. Jo) in *Keltec Challenger* rowed past, both wearing sequined Union Jack bikini tops. Truly, a 'top' effort. I was so pleased that someone had done something interesting. Each crew just seemed excited and relieved to finally be getting under way after all the hard work.

The supporters' ferry left the quay to give us all a good send-off. The Troika crowd looked fantastic and outshone the other supporters by far (although I may be biased), wearing blue Troika team tops and waving Troika blue balloons. Hayley played 'Row, row, row your boat' on her trumpet and the others sang along and held up placards which read, TROIKA, ROW YOUR BOAT.

I was so proud of them. They had made it possible for us to get to the start line, and deserved to enjoy their day thoroughly after all their hard work and sacrifices for our cause.

The start line was an imaginary line between *Challenge Yacht 24* and the harbour wall. We were able to get *Troika* into a great position next to the yacht. I 'flashed back' to a moment in a bar with Sir Chay Blyth sometime before, when he had described his amazement at watching the rowing boats in 1997 jostling for a good start position. He thought this was comical when they still had 3,000 miles to row. He'll be telling the same story in the bar again after this, I thought, since it was no different in 2001.

Within minutes of the starter hooter it was obvious which crews had elected to take the straight-line route to Barbados, and which were heading south in an attempt to pick up the strong prevailing trade winds. Within half an hour the fleet had dispersed so quickly that we could hardly see any of the other crews. It wasn't until Chay and the directors from Ward Evans, the race sponsors, sailed over to us that we knew which position we were in. Chay was bouncing up and down on the bow, gesticulating wildly towards Barbados, shouting, 'You're in fourth place!' He had always been a wonderful encouragement to our team, in part due to his friendship with Hayley, who had worked for him for five years. I didn't quite know whether to take 'fourth place' seriously, but Chay's leaping up and down convinced me!

As we rowed on, I felt pleased – but not completely surprised – at our early placing. I had always been confident that we could make the boat move fast, but we had a long way to go. I just hoped that we could keep it up. I watched two pilot whales swimming on the surface in the distance and felt enormously satisfied. I took the pair to be a good omen of all the great experiences we were bound to have along the way.

The supporters' boats finally turned and headed for the harbour. Andrew and I were alone at last – together. I didn't know then that it wouldn't be long before I would stand watching another boat turn and head away from me, this time carrying Andrew.

Then I would be very much alone.

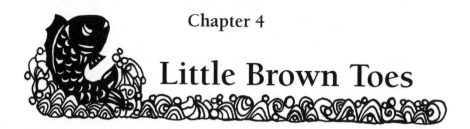

Chapter 4

Little Brown Toes

'As you are rowing across the Atlantic looking down at your little brown toes, ask yourself, "Am I the happiest I could possibly be?"'

Sir Chay Blyth

Almost as soon as Andrew had left the boat, I asked myself Chay's question again. I had considered it many times, but it seemed crucial to ask it again at that moment: 'Am I the happiest I could possibly be?' I took a good look at my exceptionally brown toes, thrilled that my answer was a resounding 'Yes!'

As Andrew sailed away, I didn't know what to do with myself, so I did what I always do and called Hayley. Our conversation was typical of those we'd had throughout our childhood and teenage years, with Hayley, the (ten-minutes) older and wiser one giving reassurance to her 'little' sister.

'Hayley, it's me.'

'Hi, little one. Has the yacht reached you yet?'

'Yes – and it's left. I'm watching Andrew sailing away now.'

'What are you doing talking to me? At least wait until he's gone!'

'I didn't know what to do with myself.'

'You feeling OK?'

'I'm fine. Actually I'm feeling really positive – excited'.

'That's good – you'd better start rowing, then.'

'OK.'

'Call me later, after it's dark, if you get scared.'

'Thanks, Hayley-Bailey.'

If in doubt, call a sister. Preferably a twin one.

I took up the oars. Those first few strokes on my own felt good. I kept looking over my shoulder at the yacht carrying Andrew away as it became an increasingly small sail in the distance. It seemed almost surreal. When it finally disappeared over the horizon, I said to myself, 'Well, here I am, on my own on a small rowing boat in the Atlantic.'

I knew that the first day alone would be fine but was unsure how I would cope with the nights. I'm quite scared of the dark, so I was expecting the first night to be a challenge, but there were considerably fewer heart palpitations than I had expected. I had this sense of invincibility that I hoped would last for all the nights to follow, a feeling largely developed after days of visualisation and mental rehearsal. I had spent hours rehearsing positively that I would be strong and invincible on my own and this was paying dividends. The skills I had learned with the GB dragon boat squad were proving to be very useful. Our coach, Griff, had taught us how to take on a new persona to elicit a positive mental state. He would encourage us to take on pseudonyms such as 'Warrior Princess' to conjure up feelings of power and rid us of our weaker, everyday labels. So, I was transformed from 'Debra the rower' into 'Debra, Warrior of the Waves'!

The next morning Leigh updated the website, telling everyone that I had continued solo. He also explained that I could receive text messages on my satellite phone and asked people to send words of encouragement. The response was phenomenal. Hundreds of people sent encouraging messages:

✉

Debs, Words cannot say how proud I
am of you for carrying on alone
across that big ocean. Love SIMON

✉

Dear Debs, Good for you. I was
moved to tears. Wot a hard decision
for A and you. Thinking of U lots.
U can do it. Much love from us all.
Pip

✉

Hi Debs just heard about Andrew —
glad to hear you're still going for
it — ATTAGIRL! Best wishes, Martin
Ward

✉

Keep at it girl! My utmost respect
for going it alone. I flew back
from US yesterday & thought of you
down there in the dark somewhere.
Liz (TwRC)

I spoke to my mother for the first time later that day. She was amazed to hear from me and kept repeating over and over, 'I love you'; 'I'm so proud of you'; 'You're so clever.' Mum is not at ease on the telephone, so her words were extra special. To my relief, she sounded confident in my ability and not too worried about me. I also received my first phone call from another boat in the race. Simon from *UniS Voyager* and his Hungarian partner Istvan called to check that I was OK on my own. I was so touched.

It was only on my return to England at the end of my adventure that I would read Andrew's response to what had happened:

Andrew's diary update

On the one hand, it's like waking up from a really bad nightmare. When your body can still feel the after-effects but you know that the threat is gone.

On the other, the nightmare goes on. Three-and-a-half years of effort and I couldn't do it. I still don't know quite how I feel about that. Disappointed obviously, but the one positive thought I have to hold on to is that, unlike other times when I've stopped doing something, only to think the very next instant that I should have continued, I haven't experienced one moment of doubt since I got on this yacht that it was the right thing to do. I think and hope as time passes that I will look on all of this as an insight into myself that few get to have, as well as appreciating some of the good bits we went through.

In the meantime, though, Debra is still out there and it looks as though she's going to give it a go. Part of me wishes she would knock it on the head and we could spend a month sailing together across the Atlantic in the yacht. I try to imagine what we could salvage from the boat and how long it would take us to pay off all our debts. But then I imagine what it will be like if she makes it – how happy she will be, how proud I will be, what an extraordinary story it will make – and I think . . . please God, look after her.

That evening I struggled to keep the boat straight in the waves. Inevitably a wave caught *Troika* at an odd angle and tipped her up. I was thrown from my rowing seat against the safety wire, and my neck took the bulk of the force against the plastic-covered metal line. I immediately developed a headache and had to crawl into the cabin to lie down.

I realised that if something serious had happened, there would have been no one to help me. If I had been knocked unconscious, the race HQ would not have known to send a safety yacht. But there was no point dwelling on the what-ifs. I understood the risks and simply had to rehearse mentally for any eventuality. The safety yacht was still relatively close, but I knew there were times ahead when it wouldn't be. It was time to start fending for myself. I had never felt so in control of my own life.

I reflected that in general my solo adventure had started positively. I felt as if I had already surpassed everyone's expectations, as I was certain that many were convinced I wouldn't last more than a day or two.

Perhaps I became too self-assured, because on the fifth night I had a complete change of heart. While having dinner, I watched some rather large fish doing laps of the boat, obviously enjoying swimming in the glow of my navigation light. At first, it was reassuring to have them there. I figured they would be unlikely to play around so casually if any sizable 'beasties from the deep' were nearby. They stayed with me as I rowed into the night until a significant 'beastie', maybe six foot long, joined them. I had previously been eagerly awaiting the return of the moon to lighten the darkness, but that night I wished it would go again. Moonlight reflects off the pale skin of the big creatures and makes them shimmer ominously under the surface of the water. When they swim fast, they leave a trail of darting phosphorescence in their wake, like an underwater lightning bolt. Had the moon not been out, I probably wouldn't have noticed them. Proof that ignorance can be bliss!

As I watched the bolt of lightning hurtle towards the side of the boat directly in line with where I was sitting, I hoped I was witnessing a dolphin rather than a shark, but once again my thinking was wishful. I couldn't get out of my head the *Jaws* movie flashbacks of sharks gnawing through the side of boats. In more logical moments I told myself that sharks attack only if provoked, but this would lead me to a whole new line of concern over whether the splashing in and out of my oars could be provoking them. I began to drop the blades into the water only lightly, causing as little splash as possible – just in case.

It may seem irrational in the light of day, but when you're alone in the dark in a very small boat made of plywood, hundreds of miles from dry land and deprived of sleep, it's very hard to be rational about such things! Eventually I was so scared that I began having palpitations and scrambled for the cabin, where I hid, petrified, until dawn broke.

My invincibility gone, I had to accept that nights were not going to be my favourite part of being alone at sea. The twelve daylight hours were brilliant, but the nights were altogether different.

I had spoken to Hayley on the satellite phone about the phrase 'choose your attitude'. We had considered that each one of us has the opportunity to choose the attitude we approach each new day with. An important part of my success was connected to choosing a more positive attitude towards the nights. I regarded them as dark and evil hours that fed, rather too successfully, my doubts and fears. So, on subsequent nights, I focused on my new choice of attitude, and it certainly seemed to make a difference. Listening to loud music also helped to block out the mysterious sounds of night. In the dark, with minimal vision, other senses go into overdrive, particularly hearing. Every splashing wave raised my heart rate, but when I couldn't hear the noises the problem was eliminated.

Even so, nothing could beat that moment when the light started to sneak onto the horizon. As dawn approached it was hard not to feel reborn – as if the light of a new day was bringing with it a new vigour for life.

I became increasingly reliant on music, and not just at night.

Listening to it made each two-hour rowing shift enjoyable and helped it pass quickly. I had a Personal Juke Box on board. It's a similar size to a Walkman but is essentially just a hard drive with the capacity to store up to a hundred CDs. I managed to load about forty onto the hard drive before I left England. The music was subdivided into wide-ranging sets. In the mornings I listened to mellow music while the sun was coming up: David Gray, Dido, Sting or James Taylor. When I hit a hyperactive patch during the day, I bopped around to Ibiza club mixes, garage and R&B or pop. Then at night I blasted out rock to keep out the sounds of the night: Red Hot Chili Peppers, Train, Lenny Kravitz and Toploader.

Completing my first week alone at sea was a great achievement. In the previous 48 hours I had begun to feel much more settled and had worked out a routine that suited my new solo status. Essentially, it meant interspersing rests between rowing shifts to allow me to complete 12 hours of rowing in a 24-hour period. Rowing for two hours, then resting for two hours, as Andrew and I had intended to do, on a rotation basis, would have meant completing half of my rowing shifts in the dark. As this was not ideal once I was alone, I changed the routine to row for two hours, then rest for only one hour, so that I could cover more shifts in daylight.

Daily routine

05.00 Wake-up call – Please tell me I've drifted 20 nautical miles SW during the night, GPS.
05.30 Row One – Ding, ding, round one.
07.30 Breakfast – 'Full English and the papers, please.'
08.30 Row Two – This beats commuting!
10.30 Mid-morning break – Whose turn to make elevenses?
11.30 Row Three – Tan fast, row the Atlantic!
13.30 Lunch – Too hot to trot, let alone cook.
14.30 Row Four – . . . *si, si, muy bueno!*
16.30 Tea break – One lump or two?
17.30 Row Five – The last of the day's rays.

> 19.30 Dinner – Shall I have beef stew, beef stew, or beef stew?
> 20.30 Row Six – Let the stargazing commence.
> 22.30 Night break – Will I make it to Row Seven?
> 23.00 Row Seven – Not going to the pub tonight, then?
> 01.00 Secure boat – Tucking *Troika* in for the night.
> 01.30–05.00 Sleep – 'I see no ships' – hopefully . . .

Good job I stuck to my daily routine rather than Pete's or I would never have made it!

✉

Pete King Daily Diary: 8 a.m. pies. 9 a.m. pies. 10 a.m. pies. 11 a.m. pies. 12 a.m. pies. 1 p.m. pies. 2 p.m. pies. 3 p.m. more pies. 4 p.m. sleep

The first task of the day was always to massage my fingers from their locked state. Twelve hours of rowing a day would lock them into a cupped position, as if I were still gripping the oars.

The ache in the joints and muscles was horrendous. I couldn't do anything until I got my fingers moving!

✉

Debra, don't worry. Curled fingers will come in very useful for holding glasses of rum etc in Barbados! B w Bernard

I would switch on the GPS to check my position, and how far I had been blown during my sleep period. Then I prepared for Row One. I was always tired. During the first session back at the oars, my body felt as if I had gone eight rounds in the ring with Lennox Lewis. But I generally enjoyed it, as I was rewarded with a sunrise in the last ten minutes of the shift.

During breakfast, I would delight in the sky's changing colours as I drank my hot chocolate, ate shortbread and breakfast bars. This rest period was my main navigation time. I filled in the ship's logbook with details of the weather and my position, but plotted my position on the chart only every five days.

The trade winds, which were supposed to be assisting my progress towards Barbados, had not yet arrived, so my progress was painfully slow. To cover just a few millimetres on the Atlantic chart I would have to 'save up' totals from several days. It was depressing to roll out the whole chart in front of me and see the vast expanse of the ocean between my position, just off Africa, and Barbados on the other side.

I soon learned a simple trick to ease my mind: I rolled up the chart so that when I next pulled it out I would have to unroll it from the Africa side, unrolling it only as far as I had travelled. My focus was then on how far I had *come* rather than how far there was left to *go* to reach Barbados.

Once the chart was rolled up, I would switch on the satellite phone, as I did at the start of every rest period, desperately hoping to receive some text messages. It was always a real disappointment if there weren't any. I was left feeling alone and stranded. Luckily, this rarely happened. Usually I would receive messages that would have me either crying with laughter or humbled and feeling very supported and cared for. Text messages, even those from my close family members and friends, never made me feel homesick. They were always just the reassurance I needed.

Once I had copied the text messages into a notebook, I would write an account of the previous day's events. I thoroughly enjoyed this; it was never a chore. Putting my experiences and feelings into words helped me keep things into perspective. I was also able to keep track of my health and wellbeing. I never seemed to find the time to have these quiet moments of reflection when on dry land.

Back in London, to say that I lived life in the fast lane would be an understatement. My mind was constantly preoccupied with the next task, before I had even finished the one I was working on. So it was wonderful to have the time really to consider how I was doing and how I was feeling, without the distractions I faced back home. I was learning more and more about myself each day.

By Row Two my body had generally woken up a bit, and the sun would still be relatively cool. It was a good time to row. During the mid-morning break, after some snacks, there were always jobs to be done: washing my night-time clothes, sorting out food, positioning the solar panels and making fresh water. I carried 150 litres of water on board, in the hull of the boat as ballast, but it could be drunk only in an emergency. So, for day-to-day survival, I was reliant on my trusty water purifier powered by solar panels. It converted saltwater to fresh drinking water, a fairly slow process, taking approximately two hours to produce ten litres. So not a drop could be wasted. After all that effort I was left with a liquid that *looked* like water, but had a slightly brackish taste to it. Some days it tasted better than others, and mostly I grew accustomed to it, but when I got back to dry land and had my first taste of bottled water I realised how nasty my 'purified' sea water tasted!

In the daytime I always rowed naked (after all there was no one around to see!), not because I'm a naturist or an exhibitionist but because it was the only way to prevent getting sores on my bottom. Sitting on a small hard rowing seat in thirty-odd degrees centigrade for twelve hours a day, covered in salt crystals and wearing shorts that cause sweating, was a guaranteed way to get sores, boils or chafing on my bottom. With added infection, the pain of sitting on any surface, let alone a hard rowing seat, would be excruciating.

This was something we had planned meticulously to avoid. Andrew and I had approached our boat builder and asked if he would take plaster casts of our bottoms – probably not a request he gets every day! From these he made fibreglass moulds to produce the perfectly fitted rowing seat. We then covered the seats in sheepskin. Letting the skin breathe and using the sheepskin seat covers was a definite 'bottom saver' but on the odd occasion Sudacrem emollient certainly came to the rescue.

Many of the crews rowed naked, and those who didn't soon learned the error of their ways! As more and more crews called me, I started to hear hilarious stories from other nudist boats. In this sense, going with my husband had been a definite advantage. Climbing into the cabin through the small hatch, which faces the person who is rowing, was apparently the worst 'eyewitness account'. There is no dignified, legs-together way to complete *that* manoeuvre!

During Row Three, the last few hours before lunch, it often became unbearably hot. I would drink by the clock, sipping every fifteen minutes to avoid dehydration. I'd slap on sun cream and start to feel as if I were frying. All the lunches we packed required cooking, but the last thing I felt like doing was sitting by a hot gas cooker, so I often skipped lunch and snacked instead. As I completely lost my appetite at sea and had to force myself to eat, I often ate as little as a small bag of mixed fruit and nuts for lunch.

I didn't really crave any particular foods or drinks at first, although I felt quite differently after three months of repeatedly consuming the same ones! By then the only thing I craved was a more varied diet. I've never been into chocolate and don't have any particular food 'vices', which probably made it easier to cope.

At the end of Row Three I would call Hayley, or one of the support team, to give a report of my progress. Every third day I dictated my diary down the phone to update the website. The support team were brilliant at sending out the updates. They were initially for friends and family, but grew in popularity. Hundreds of people from around the world began to sign up. The *Troika Transatlantic* website was a huge success. My brother-in-law Leigh committed hundreds of hours to it. It contained information about our team and sponsors, the boat, equipment, the tracking system (showing the positions of all the teams), a forum for supporters to chat online and the all-important diary updates. From these, Leigh set up a link to the text-messaging page of the Iridum satellite-phone company website. This allowed the supporters to respond directly to what I was writing in the updates.

Row Four was my Spanish lesson! One of the many goals I set myself during the challenge was to learn how to speak Spanish. An hour and a half of listening to a CD of a Spanish class made time pass *rápidamente*. I had an eight-CD Spanish course, which proved to be stimulating and quite effective, although the greater challenge was practising my conversation without anyone to talk to. I happened to mention this in one of my diary updates – I should have expected the response that followed.

⊠

Hi Debra. I am Manuela. I'm from Uzla but I live in Dubai. Let's practice your Spanish okay? Como Estas? Como te sientes? Espero que bien y con mucho animo. Bye Manuela.

During the afternoon tea break (minus the tea – it tasted horrible when made with brackish water and was just too hot for the conditions) I would read, or write my diary. Andrew and I had allowed ourselves the treat of taking one book each, aside from an oh-so-handy fish reference book. Our French friend, Christelle, was full of recommendations. For me she recommended *Memoirs of a Geisha* by Arthur Golden and Andrew a book in French. Looking back, I suppose this wasn't a brilliant idea, as I can't read French. However, the novel about a celebrated geisha was a fascinating read and taught me much about the traditions of Japanese culture. For the first two months it was the only book I had on board – I still enjoyed it after the third time of reading it.

Sometimes I would nap like a cat before starting Row Five – my last two hours of rowing in daylight as the sun set at the end of the shift. It immediately went cool after the sun had dropped below the horizon, so I would pull my clothes on before preparing yet another sumptuous feast of beef stew and dumplings. My appetite often returned a little after the sun had gone down, so for dinner I cooked myself a big meal to make up for all the food I should have eaten during the day. Even then, I knew it wasn't enough.

After dinner came the highlight of my day: Andrew. Even if I could only call him on the Challenge yacht, it was a way of having him in the boat with me for a short while. Unfortunately, it wasn't until the end that we found out that calls cost £8 a minute! We ran up over £12,000 worth of satellite-phone bills – but they were worth it. Having Andrew's support and encouragement in those first few weeks on my own was vital.

It would take me about ten minutes to get into rowing in the dark at the start of Row Six, and often much longer if there was no moon, or the cloud cover was thick. To stop myself searching for shapes in the waves, I would turn the music up and chant to myself, 'Keep your eyes in the boat, Debra.' If I saw an ominous shape in the water, I would throw my head back and concentrate on the stars, trying not to think about what might be swimming beneath me.

The stars are so bright above the Atlantic. The night sky is breathtaking. Without the glare of street lights, the Milky Way and other systems can be seen in all their glory. Sometimes the sky looked so full of stars I expected it to burst at any minute.

It was the shooting stars, though, that really held my attention, streaking across the blackness in their thousands. The larger ones left glowing trails arching across the skies – just like the start of a Disney movie.

Every night, heavy dew fell on the boat, preventing me from sitting outside comfortably during my night break; but, if I got into the cabin, I risked falling asleep. After a 5 a.m. start and ten hours of rowing a boat weighing the best part of a ton, it's hard not to do so. But, if I succumbed to the sleep fairies, I would find it almost impossible to get up for Row Seven. Consequently, it was the shift that I (accidentally) skipped the most. There was little incentive to climb out of my warm, dry cabin at 11 p.m. for that one.

I was completely exhausted by that point. It took every bit of mental strength I had to drag myself back to the oars, where I occasionally fell asleep. It amazed me that I could still do so in a sitting position, while gripping the oars and with seawater splashing over me – but it happened! Sometimes I would wake up at the oars, startled to discover that I had been asleep for over half an hour.

Before I could go to sleep at the end of Row Seven, I had to tie up the oars and secure everything on the deck. I was then up frequently during the 'sleep' session to scan the horizon for ships, and check the compass and wind direction. All too soon it was 5 a.m., the alarm was going off, and it was time to start the whole thing all over again. Just occasionally when I was particularly exhausted I would fall asleep the second my head touched the pillow and not wake up again until I heard the alarm. This would send me into a complete panic.

⊠

Debs. B careful tonight. I worry about U sleeping for 4 hours without scanning the horizon 4 ships. No yacht would do that. 143, HB

Sleeping in such a small craft on the ocean is quite an art. The four-inch acrylic canvas-and-foam cushions that covered the cabin floor were my bed, but remained in place throughout. They had to – there was nowhere else to put them.

No matter what the sea state, the boat was always in motion. When lying down – provided it was not excessively rough – my body moved with the boat. Unfortunately, the same cannot be said for my internal organs, which felt as if they were sloshing around within my torso – a disconcerting feeling. When the waves grew larger, the problem became how to avoid rolling from one side of the cabin to the other in my sleep. As the boat was forced over by the big swells, I would be thrown against the side wall of the cabin, my body weight not great enough to pin me to the bed.

I tried all manner of things to combat these problems. Sleeping on my front so that my internal organs were squashed into the cushions certainly helped the sloshing, but defying gravity when the boat was rolling was more of a challenge! In moderate swells, sleeping in the recovery position prevented me from bowling around too much. I also packed clothing along either side of my body to block myself on to the spot. But when it got very rough the only action available was to brace myself between the two side walls of the cabin by sleeping across its width, my feet against one wall and my back and head against the other. I could achieve this only because I am so small. It has to be said that none of these tricks encouraged a good night's sleep, but the constant exhaustion helped me forget about the discomfort very nicely.

My set routine seemed to work quite well but felt like *Groundhog Day* at times. After ten days alone I was really into the swing of it. Thoroughly happy and with my contentment growing, I then had my first truly awful day. I suppose I should have been pleased: one day out of 24 at seas wasn't bad, but it was impossible to see it that way at the time. It was one of those days when everything seemed to go wrong and whatever I did seemed only to make things worse.

I had attempted to throw some of Andrew's powdered food over board, since I didn't need it all and it weighed a vast amount. It was a blustery day and I wasn't thinking. If I had been, I would have realised that the powdered food would be dispersed everywhere by the wind. As I poured it over the side, it blew up into my eyes, so I had to shut them tight. Once the container was empty I opened my eyes to see what resembled a scene from a winter wonderland. A film of white powder covered every surface, not only on the deck, but also in the cabin, because the hatch was tied wide open.

It had coated my bed, clothes, pillow – everything and every-where. To make matters worse, the dried food did exactly what it is designed to do when mixed with water: it expanded rapidly! I wasn't too concerned about the deck – I could throw buckets of water over that and wash it out of the scuppers – but the inside was a real problem. I tried pulling one of the cushions out of the cabin to brush off the powder but, as if on command, a wave splashed over the deck and hit the cushion full on. The cushion immediately started to sprout goo, like bacteria growing out of control, and it doubled in size every second. Everything I did made the situation worse. In desperation I screamed, 'Give me a break' at the sprouting cushions.

I shut the hatch and turned my attention to getting the exterior sorted out first. As I struggled to clear up the deck, waves were landing on my head, soaking me to the skin. I had reached breaking point. I looked up to take some deep breaths and count to ten to calm myself. I stopped at three, as my heart lurched for a completely unexpected reason. What I saw did nothing to induce calm.

A huge container ship was bearing down on my position, its steel hull munching through the ocean between us. *Troika* cowered in fear. The bow wave from the ship was being thrown 40 feet in the air, curling over in a mass of violently foaming white water. It was so close that there wasn't time for the captain to respond to a call on the VHF to make him aware of my existence. In a moment of cutting fear I realised that, even if the ship didn't hit me, the bow wave would tear the boat apart. Those on board the vast steel monster wouldn't hear the shattering of *Troika*'s plywood hull over the thunderous noise of the engine, let alone my screams for help.

Surely this was it. Forget mental rehearsal. I was going to die.

Seconds seemed like hours as the monster ploughed onward, slicing through the water. I stood motionless with fear, but as I looked closer at the bow wave, my distress began to ease. It might, it just might . . .

I realised with the beginnings of relief, that I could see the bow wave on the starboard side more than the port side. This meant that the ship was at an angle to *Troika*. Its course must have been a few degrees different from mine. A few life-saving degrees. I realised it wasn't going to hit us. *Troika* could breathe easy. The ship would simply roar by, as if we were a speck of dirt.

I sat watching it pass, feeling mentally broken and alone. I felt helpless. Hopeless. The crew didn't even know I was there. I don't know how long I sat there without moving. Certainly, long after the ship was out of sight. I was overwhelmed with the aftermath of terrifying emotion, and completely exhausted.

Getting that low in the middle of the ocean is isolating to an extreme. There is no one to pick you up and tell you it will be OK or to offer a much-needed hug. No one, even, to share the fear and doubt. I knew I couldn't afford to feel sorry for myself, and that in reality the highs outweighed the lows. But lows that deep were difficult to climb out of and left me vulnerable.

Normally, bad times would be helped by a visualisation exercise. It was always the same one. I would imagine rowing into Port St Charles, Barbados, where my family and friends would be lined up on the quay to greet me. I would go through the scene in minute detail: what each person would be wearing, how it would feel to hug each one and what I would say. I imagined the sounds, the smells, the colours, but most of all the enormous sense of achievement. Soon I would be grinning to myself like an idiot! Unfortunately, the power of that wonderful picture was not nearly enough to help me on that difficult day. My confidence evaporated and with it my enthusiasm. I started to think about how much time I had to go before I reached Barbados. I knew I had at least another two months of being on my own and scared.

I called Hayley and told her that I was thinking of giving up and calling the safety yacht. I was crying so hard that I could hardly get the words out. I said I wanted to be home. That I felt I couldn't handle the pressure of fending for myself in such a vast ocean where potential dangers were beyond my control.

'Don't give up,' said Hayley. 'You're capable of so much more mental hardship than this.'

That one sentence was so powerful. I don't know if I believed it at the time – and, frankly, it was easy for her to say as she sat in her cosy living room back in England! But the more I thought about it, the more I realised she was right. I wasn't about to die, I wasn't in pain, I had food and I had water. I was OK.

She had given me hope. During the night shift of that disastrous day, a piece of music by the New Radicals really spoke to me. 'You Get What you Give' became a significant part of my adventure:

> *But when the night is falling*
> *And you cannot find the light*
> *If you feel your dream is dying*
> *Hold tight*

You've got the music in you
Don't let go
Don't give up

Each time this chorus was sung – particularly the line 'don't give up' – I felt my determination come creeping steadily back. I knew with growing confidence that I was not going to be beaten by one bad day. I felt empowered once again. Nothing was going to stand in my way. I knew there would be more bad days, but I'd take them on one at a time – and win.

I began to see tankers and container ships often, thankfully none quite as close as the steel monster. I had pushed south on the advice of John Searson, the solo rower from 1997, to avoid a low-pressure weather system, and inadvertently rowed into a shipping lane for the Cape Verde Islands. Clever of me, don't you think?

By the last day of October I was free of the shipping lane and had managed to avoid the worst of the headwinds in the low-pressure system. Some of my male counterparts to the north had not fared so well. John's meteorological advice had yet again been invaluable. The headwinds I experienced were light but still causing me to drift backwards every rest period.

I was losing one nautical mile for every two I gained. As I rowed sluggishly into the wind, I couldn't help watching every nautical second that clocked on the GPS. I had to work hard for every inch of forward advancement, and it was soul-destroying to witness them slipping away each time I stopped to rest and drifted backwards. The boat felt heavy in these conditions and caused much stiffness and aching the following day – but at least I was making some headway.

The vast amount of mental strength and determination I seemed to be finding within myself was a daily source of wonder, but not something for which I could take all the credit. While at university I had studied sport psychology as part of my degree course, but it wasn't until I met Griff, the coach of the GB dragon boat team, that I fully understood its power. In particular the usefulness of focusing on different quotations, phrases or sayings, in order to elicit different physical responses.

Kia kaha (Maori for 'stay strong') had been sent to me by a supporter in New Zealand. I used this saying to calm me down when ever I felt panicked or unable to cope with a situation. I would inhale deeply, filling my lungs completely, and would exhale through the words '*Kia kaha*', squeezing the last breath from the depths of my lungs as I ended on the 'haaaaaaa'.

I began to receive quotations, poems and Bible verses, useful sayings and phrases via text messages from those who were following my voyage. Every word was a huge source of mental stimulation and encouragement. They became integrated into my daily routines and were vital to the success of my day.

At breakfast, as I watched the sun rise, I would start by focusing on those three words – 'choose your attitude'. I fixed them to the hatch in front of my rowing position so that I could focus on them throughout the day. It would have been so easy to sit at the oars being negative about the monotony, tiredness, awful food and lack of company, but it would have done me no good at all.

So I started each day trying to be positive about all the great things that might happen in the next 24 hours. I imagined seeing lots of great wildlife, achieving my best mileage to date, learning a few more Spanish verbs or taking the time to be peaceful for a while. I soon realised that I could make the most of what was to come only if I approached the day with a high level of optimism and with a positive attitude.

Once I had chosen an attitude with which to approach my new day (the 'choice' of a negative attitude was not an option!), I read two poems, 'Sea Fever' (John Masefield) and 'A life on the Ocean Wave' (Epes Sargent), sent in via text messages from friends. These two old poems brilliantly illustrate the beauty of ocean life. Reading them reminded me to look for something beautiful and positive in my day.

Sea Fever

I must go down to the sea again, to the lonely sea and the sky,
And all I ask is a tall ship and a star to steer her by,
And the wheel's kick and the wind's song and the white sail's
    shaking,
And a grey mist on the sea's face and a grey dawn breaking.

I must down to the sea again, for the call of the running tide
Is a wild call and a clear call that may not be denied;
And all I ask is a windy day with the white clouds flying,
And the flung spray and the blown spume, and the sea-gulls
    crying.

I must down to the sea again, to the vagrant gypsy life.
To the gull's way and the whale's way where the wind's like a
    whetted knife;
And all I ask is a merry yarn from a laughing fellow-rover,
And quiet sleep and a sweet dream when the long trick's over.

A Life on the Ocean Wave

A life on the ocean wave,
A home on the rolling deep,
Where the scattered waters rave,
And the winds their revels keep!
Like an eagle caged, I pine
On this dull, unchanging shore:
Oh! give me the flashing brine,
The spray and the tempest's roar!
Once more on the deck I stand
Of my own swift-gliding craft:
Set sail! farewell to the land!
The gale follows fair abaft.
We shoot through the sparkling foam
Like an ocean-bird set free —
Like the ocean-bird, our home
We'll find far out on the sea.

The land is no longer in view,
The clouds have begun to frown;
But with a stout vessel and crew,
We'll say, Let the storm come down!
And the song of our hearts shall be,
While the winds and the waters rave,
A home on the rolling sea!
A life on the ocean wave!

I had a whole catalogue of quotations to motivate, inspire or get me through the hard times. I often used 'This too will pass', which was sent to me by a number of people. 'My eyes are an Ocean in which my dreams are reflected' (Anna Uhlich) became particularly important, along with 'It is good to have an end to journey towards, but it is the journey that matters in the end' (Ursula Le Guin).

Newton's Third Law of Motion kept whirling around in my head (well, more cerebral than counting sheep!). 'For every action there is an equal and opposite reaction'. My dragon boat coach, Griff, liked this one, explaining that the faster and harder the blade is pulled through the water, the faster the boat will travel.

I liked to think that for every ounce of effort I put into life at sea there was also an equal return on that effort. As I thought of Newton's Law, I tried not to set limits on my mental effort. If I did, I found they became barriers in my mind that prevented me from going a step further in whatever I was doing. It was too easy to believe I would not be able to achieve something because that 'step' was beyond the mental limit I had set myself.

Every day I learned new lessons about myself. Perhaps one of the most powerful was the lesson that I was capable of so much more than I believed I was. As I pushed myself far, far beyond any limits I had previously set, I found I could still achieve and that the results were deeply satisfying.

My overriding feeling as I rowed further across the Atlantic was what a fantastic ocean it is. As I reflected on those first few weeks alone, I realised that, despite the momentary wobbles and low or lonely patches, the Atlantic always seemed to find ways to seduce and enchant me again – often through the simple things that we just don't get to do every day, like rowing naked in the rain!

Raindrops are big and fat in the Atlantic. Rain seems to come in two forms – bizarrely random or consistently hard. Some days I'd be rowing along in the bright sunshine when raindrops would suddenly fall from what I thought was a clear blue sky. I'd look up to discover a wafer-thin cloud directly above me. The sun would continue to shine while fat drops fell on my birthday suit. It was quite a sensation for the few minutes it lasted, so I would dash to put the Red Hot Chili Peppers song 'Naked in the Rain' on the Personal Juke Box to 'live the moment'. I would try not to wince as every drop that hit my skin felt more like a cupful!

The consistently hard rain often started during the early hours of the morning and could only be described as torrential. It would rain so hard that the 'inner sanctum' of my cabin would be penetrated. Rain would work its way in through the holes that had been drilled for the solar panel's wires. They were encased in watertight joints but the rain was persistent in its attack and eventually found a way in. I couldn't blame it – it was horrid out there! The noise of the rain driving against the plywood cabin was thunderous. With an occasional bright flash of sheet lightning thrown in, it could be quite dramatic – especially at night. The rain was brilliant at washing away any niggling negative feelings I had. I loved to be wrapped up in my Musto waterproofs, fleecy collar pulled up over my ears, rowing along through the rain. The spray on my face was so refreshing it made me feel truly alive.

A rainstorm was also the only time when I would be free from the salt that custed on my skin. I gave up washing after a few weeks, as there really didn't seem much point. If I washed, I would soon be covered in saltwater again and I couldn't afford to waste precious fresh water.

The air was so pure in the Atlantic. I soon began to notice that my skin had never been so healthy or my pores so free from grime

– a stark contrast to what I was used to back in southwest London! I didn't seem to smell too bad either – but I may have deceived myself on that front! I became very used to my own scent and, with no one else around to have a sniff, I suppose there really was no way of knowing. It did cross my mind that it would be embarrassing to step onto the quayside in Barbados and throw my arms around Andrew, only to spoil the moment for him with my excessive BO! I decided I'd wash the day before I finished – just to be on the safe side.

'How did you go to the loo?' is the one question that British people always ask me – what is this British fascination with toilet talk! Thankfully, there is not a lot to tell. I had a simple 'Bucket-and-chuck-it' system, which was most effective – unless the wind got up and until I ran out of toilet paper. I soon learned that the 'chuck-it' phase of the process was best not carried out into a headwind. There is something quite lovely about having an open-air toilet with such a beautiful view. All in all, I would highly recommend it!

Chapter 5

With a Little Help from My Friends

Sunrise was my favourite part of the day. I loved the way the shades of pinks and reds crept upwards, sending my 360-degree water-world horizon into an excited glow. The water all around me would turn candyfloss pink and the light would bounce off it as if millions of diamonds were floating on the surface. Listening to music that was not in a hurry to go anywhere seemed to slow time, making each moment last longer.

It was during one of these sunrise moments that I found freedom from the hurt and pain of Dad's death. It had been gnawing away at me for two years, yet I hadn't realised just how much pain was buried inside until it had finally gone. I had been trapped in a world of self-pity and sorrow because I couldn't get past one major issue: that Dad was not going to be around to share in my future, and how much I wished he could be.

The 'I wish' syndrome is a dangerous one and I suppose it stayed with me because I tied it to myself, dragging it everywhere, especially during the time between Dad's funeral and our wedding. I'd chant in my head like some Buddhist monk repeating his mantra: 'I wish Dad was alive to walk me down the aisle; I wish Dad was alive to walk me down the aisle.' Soon the 'I wish' syndrome was knotted tight by

further longings. 'I wish Dad could be around to watch his
grandchildren growing up; I wish Dad could be in Barbados to see
me finish . . .' I just couldn't break free, let go and accept that I could
have a life without him.

Then, one morning in the hours before that 'sunrise moment', as
the Atlantic darkness slowly faded away, so did all those binding
wishes. As the horizon began to glow, its warmth seemed to
permeate my very being, melting away the pain, and banishing the
darkness that had enveloped me for too long. I watched the smooth,
bright-orange sphere of the sun break over the horizon and realised
that it was time to stop dwelling on my loss and start celebrating –
celebrating Dad, his life and everything he stood for. I realised that I
could let go of him without forgetting him, that I would remember
every day his enthusiasm, his eternal optimism and his love of life –
and emulate it.

For days afterwards, I slid along a glassy surface that hardly knew
a ripple. Blue sky and white cotton-wool clouds were reflected on
the surface and everything was silent. I had never known peace and
tranquillity like it. It was as though the wide expanse of the Atlantic
had been watching me and knew that stillness and time were what I
needed. The feeling of utter contentment was enormous and would
return to me often, like a familiar friend, throughout the rest of my
journey to Barbados.

To my joy, it seemed as if Dad had joined me in the boat. I saw
him everywhere because it no longer hurt to do so. He sat with me
as I ate, saying, as he did at the end of every meal my mother ever
cooked him, 'Well, that was a gastronomic delight' – proof that he
was remarking on **Mum's** cooking and couldn't really taste my beef
stew and dumplings! I could see him lounging by the hatch while I
rowed, cold beer in his hand and a wide smile on his face. Every so
often he would turn his familiar features to the sun and shout across
to me, 'I say, isn't this lovely!' in just the way he did on *Rio Luna*
when I was younger.

The whole experience brought with it an unexpected clarity of
mind. I have never been good at recalling my childhood. Hayley has

Right: My twin sister Hayley and I, aged two. We were so incredibly identical when we were little that wearing different colours helped everyone tell the difference. I always wore pink.

Below: Aged three. Is this when it all started?

Below: Dad, Hayley and me, aged five (I'm on the right).

Far left: Proud to be wearing our Devon Tennis team tracksuits, aged twelve.

Left: Ascent of Barre des Ecrins, France, aged twenty. After this expedition I vowed never to take the easy option again.

Main photograph: My previous adventures had given me plenty of practice at 'roughing it', which helped me to adapt quickly to life on *Troika Transatlantic*.

Above: Kayaking a waterfall while at university – the more extreme the better!

Below: My lovely family: Matt, Simon, Dad, Mum, Hayley, me and Harvey the dog.

Above: Racing at the European Championships in Rome with the Great Britain Dragon Boat Team (I'm number 14).

Left: With Andrew on my graduation day in 1997.

Right: 17 July 1999 – our special day.

Top left: Andrew, Joanna and Pete. It took us days to put together the 120 x 8000 calorie day packs of food.

Left: I drove Andrew mad painting and re-painting *Troika* – I wanted her to look her best!

Below: 7 October 2001. The morning of the race had finally arrived – here we are waiting on the start line.

Above: And we're off!

Below: The best support team in the world – *(left to right)* Pete, Leigh, Hayley, Chris, Simon and Joanna.

Left: Andrew adapting *Troika Transatlantic* for my solo voyage.

Below: Alone but excited about my solo adventure.

HOOD C 24

Ward Evans Co

ROWING CHALLENGE

Above: 20 October 2001. Andrew's relief was immediate once he transferred onto the support yacht.

Below: Whales visited regularly.

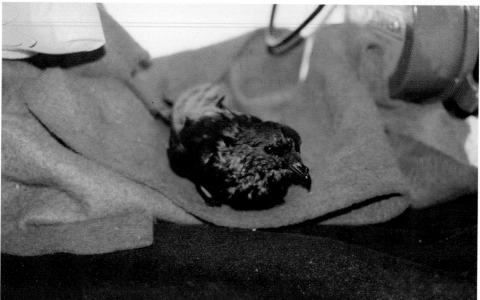

Top: My friend Barney the turtle, so called because of his barnacled face and shell.

Above: 'Squelchy' rested on board *Troika Transatlantic* for a few days and was a welcome distraction.

Photo by John Farndell

Above: Andrew sitting with skipper Lin Parker after transferring onto *Challenge Yacht 47*.

Right: The sunsets and sunrises were always breathtaking.

Above: Andrew relaxing at Cath and Thomas's house after sailing across the Atlantic.

Left: A mid-Atlantic encounter with Pete and Nikki on *Seventh Heaven*.

Above: Festive decorations from my Christmas parcel.

Right: With Woody, celebrating Christmas Day at sea.

Below: Inside the tiny cabin of *Troika Transatlantic* – my home for three-and-a-half months.

Above: Close friends and family made it clear that my finish was long overdue!

Below: A victory salute – I received the most amazing welcome at Port St Charles, Barbados.

Photo by Mark Pepper at Marinepics

Above: Precision champagne spraying by Sir Chay Blyth.

Right: That long-dreamed-of-hug from Andrew.

Below: The press pack move in!

Photo by Tim Clarke/Express Newspapers

Me and Andrew with Maritza and her staff at North Point. Flying above us is the flag she made for me.

always been able to remember much further back. In recent years, my head has been so full of business decisions and planning ahead that even the details of recent events escape me. But out on the ocean my mind was free. Released from responsibilities – my daily chores did not require much thought – I found that I could remember places and people from my past that had been buried beneath it all. I had to acknowledge that my hectic life had been casting a shadow over so many memories. It was wonderful to recall those who had shaped my life and helped me get where I was – bobbing about in a little boat in the middle of the Atlantic.

Reaching the first day of a new month – 1 November 2001 – felt great. I celebrated by allowing myself a new sheepskin seat cover to sit on while rowing. At the time my derrière was greatly relieved, as I had two salt sores that were making life quite uncomfortable, but that's what you get for sitting around the Atlantic all day! Seat-cover replacement became established as a monthly ritual. (I remember thinking as I pulled out December's new sheepskin, that I really must have been out there too long if I had monthly, as well as daily and weekly, rituals.)

Progress was painfully slow at this stage, but I didn't mind. Most days I was too busy revelling in the peace and tranquillity to worry about how slowly I was going, but the days with headwinds were frustrating and physically draining. My hands and back always took the brunt of them. It wasn't blisters on my hands that were the problem, but stiffness. Getting out of the cabin at 5.30 a.m. and taking those first few strokes into the headwinds was dark and miserable. Every muscle in my body would scream for mercy as I attempted to propel the boat into what felt like a brick wall. When I stopped for a rest, I would be blown back the single mile it had just taken me an hour to gain. It was hard not to get demoralised.

It was an odd feeling, rowing into a headwind. The resistance was so great as I heaved on the oars that I got the impression that I must be moving the boat forward. Glances at the GPS soon quashed any hopes that this was the case. When this happened, I moved quickly into damage-limitation mode and pulled out the parachute anchor, the largest of the sea anchors I had on board and by far the most effective sea anchor for turning the boat into the head wind and stopping it in its tracks.

Despite the flat calm days and occasional headwinds, I still believed that I could make it to Barbados before Christmas. I knew it would be close, but I was determined. On 3 November, I had a good look at the chart and focused on my next goal – reaching 30 degrees west by the 13th. I worked out that I just needed to do 30 miles a day for the next ten days. Surely that was possible. All I needed was the trade winds to play the game I had signed up for, and start pushing me from behind.

With every day that passed I felt more at home, almost at one, with the ocean. It was obvious that the animals felt at home with me, too. They visited frequently and seemed completely at ease with my presence. I decided that, out of all of the oceanic creatures I had observed, the sea turtles were definitely my favourite. Their inherent clumsy nature reminded me of what has affectionately become known as my occasional 'puppy-paws phase', during which I tend to knock everything over, spill or burn with ease and invariably leave my wallet in the back of a taxi. I don't know why I have these days of clumsiness, but I now realise that they are very turtle-esque.

The first sea turtle to visit I named Albert. No particular reason – he just looked like an Albert. I had never seen a turtle up close before, so I was surprised both by how Jurassic they are in appearance and how entertaining they are to watch. Albert seemed completely unbothered by my touching his shell but I made sure I kept my fingers away from his beak, which looked scarily sharp and hard. He must have thought all his birthdays and Christmases had come at once, because not only had he found a boat with tasty fresh young weed growing on the hull but the boat also moved slowly enough for him to keep up with it. I suppose I was supplying a 'meals-on-hulls' service for my new friend. When he surfaced for air he exhaled, then inhaled with such gusto that his head wobbled and he went slightly cross-eyed, reducing me to hysterical fits of giggles every time. Albert also had a particular problem with diving back under the boat after he had come up for air. He repeatedly misjudged the manoeuvre and head-butted the side of the boat, which resulted in more giggling than sympathy from me.

The night after I first met Albert I was woken at 2 a.m. by a clunking and scraping sound coming from under the boat. After each clunk the boat shuddered. Having watched and listened to Albert the day before, I realised that it was the sound of the boat rolling on to a turtle's hard shell followed by the noise of a beak scraping off weed. When I looked over the side, the Big Mac of all turtles emerged from the dark water for air. No wonder the boat had shuddered. This wasn't Albert, but a relative of his, easily over a metre long. How could I fail to be cheered by a giant turtle waking me in the middle of the night? After all, it's not something that happens back home.

✉

Hi — I'm scared to pee in the wee dark hours and with nothing scraping on my bottom but a wad of Andrex! Jooles Payne

Of all the turtles, my favourite had to be Barney, so named because of the many barnacles stuck to his shell, particularly on his bottom and around his mouth. He even had barnacle-looking lumps on his tongue. Barney was not an agile turtle.

The sea was choppy on the day we met, tossing the boat dramatically and landing on Barney with an enormous crack every time it rolled to port. Barney didn't seem to mind at all, but I became increasingly concerned about him cracking open the hull, which was, after all, constructed from plywood that was only 9 millimetres thick. Barney also removed large amounts of the blue antifoul from the hull. Every time he came up for air his shell was getting bluer and bluer. For the safety of *Troika* I decided to row away, but Barney gave chase for a full and frantic 30 minutes! I had to laugh at the ridiculousness of the scene. There I was, pulling as hard as I could but unable to shake off a big old turtle tailing me like some unskilled undercover agent. Thank goodness he gave up – eventually.

⊠

`Hey, lady. This blue paint won't`
`come off, wife will kill me when I`
`get home. Got anything to remove`
`it? Love, Barney.`

It may seem an obvious thing to say, but the Atlantic is full of fish! I kept a fish reference book on board, and often dashed into the cabin to leaf through the pictures, trying to find a match for the one I had just seen swimming by (slightly sad in a fish-spotting kind of way, but there isn't much else to do in the middle of the Atlantic and you have to get your kicks somehow!). I became quite fascinated by the statistics in that little book. On one occasion I spotted a manta ray gliding around the boat and was just thinking how graceful it was until I read that their wingspan can grow to lengths of *24 feet* – longer than the boat!

Dorados (dolphinfish) and flying fish were always around. But the flying fish didn't know that *I* was around, and became the bane of my ocean-going life. Every night during flying practice many would crash-land on the boat and, unable to get back to the water, they would suffocate. I couldn't bear to watch them flapping about and gasping for their lives, so I would pick them up and throw them overboard. The problem was that they were slimy, smelly, and left half of their scales behind in my hands. Trying to remove this scaly goo was similar to a disastrous nappy-changing incident: it got everywhere, stuck like glue, and the smell lingered long after the culprit was comfortably elsewhere. But I couldn't help acting like an attentive mother, even in the middle of the night, when I would climb out of my warm, dry cabin to perform my duty.

By contrast, I became like the child catcher from *Chitty Chitty Bang Bang* first thing in the morning. I could smell the flying fish but

I couldn't always see them, as they flew into all kinds of nooks and crannies. So I sniffed them out. The scales that they shed dried in the hot sunshine, becoming as light as a feather. Then, when the wind got up in the evening, they would be dispersed everywhere. There was nothing worse than dreamily sipping on a steaming mug of hot chocolate, only to discover a fish scale floating in it. Or finding them in my sleeping bag, or between my toes, which really infuriated me. Flying at high speeds, the fish seemed to come from nowhere. When the big ones hit me, they hurt as much as being given a dead-arm punch, just like those delivered in playgrounds worldwide. Although most of the fish were tiny and just bounced off, they could still be a nuisance, especially when I was eating or if they dropped into my lap while I was rowing naked. One suppertime such a little nuisance hit me square between the eyes, and landed, on rebound, in the bowl of pasta I was munching. Personally, I prefer tuna in my pasta!

✉

```
If I'd thought about all those
kamikaze flying fish I'd have
included a butterfly net with the
rest of the fishing gear! AMW
```

Dorados, on the other hand, are one cool species of fish. They would swim along with me for miles and miles and, helpfully, they eat flying fish. Most of them were about a metre in length and the most beautiful bright *Troika* blue, with glowing green-yellow fins and tails. Obligingly sponsor-colour-coordinated! They cleared the water at a great height as they leaped out and slammed back down in an attempt to remove parasites. Despite the size and weight of these beasties (my oh-so-handy little fish book told me they can weigh up to 40 kilos), some of them cleared two to three metres above the water level. They landed with an almighty splash, which reminded me of teaching diving to year 5s at St Margaret's School. Definitely more of a belly flop – from both groups.

One night they were going for it big time, as if they were taking part in the Dorado High Jump Championships, so I decided to try to photograph them. They stay airborne for quite some time, so I figured that if I could just get the camera pointing in vaguely the right direction, I could get a good picture. Nice idea in theory – I now have a new-found respect for wildlife photographers. Tim Welford – the Pacific rower – said that trying to take photos of whales was like the giant-panda Kit Kat advert, where, every time the photographer turns his back on the cave entrance, the pandas come out on rollerskates. My experience was very similar. Every time I set myself up to look out over the port side, I would hear a splash and turn just in time to catch a whopper landing from an epic leap on the starboard side. After this had happened a few times I switched to the starboard side, only for all of the leaping action to switch to the port side. I'm convinced it was a dorado conspiracy – 'Operation Photo Avoidance'. One of the lesser leapers was on watch, reporting back to the rest of the team. I could almost imagine the radio call: 'Bravo, this is Alpha. Target is mobile . . . now static on the port side. All stations, switch to starboard side – GO, GO, GO!'

I was often joined by fish that did not appear in my now 'not-so-handy' fish book. They had no fins on the side of their oval-shaped bodies, just a large one on their back and another on their belly. Their fins were completely out of proportion to the rest of their torso and flopped in an ungainly way from side to side. I found it almost impossible not to laugh at them as I watched them flop by. I called them 'Kissy fish' because of the noise they made when eating. They fed on the plankton floating in air bubbles on the surface of the water, which they consumed by sucking in sharply. This resulted in a surprisingly loud kissing noise. Every time they blew me a kiss, I blew them one back. Seemed only polite!

✉

Still can't imagine your lot, so am buying a goldfish. Need u to suggest names please. Love Matt & Christelle x

Andrew and I had now been apart for two weeks. I was able to speak to him daily, or, if I was feeling strong, every other day. Andrew had changed from *Challenge Yacht 24* to *Challenge Yacht 47* and he and the crew were working their way to the front of the fleet, trying to visit all of the rowing boats along the way. By this point there were more than a thousand miles between the front and the back runners and finding each boat, rowing in solitude, was becoming increasing difficult.

I was concerned that Andrew would find visiting all of the crews hard, as most of them wouldn't know that he had got off and I had carried on alone until they saw him sailing towards them, but this didn't seem to be the case. He was enjoying visiting the other rowers and they were all supportive and understanding. I'm sure every one of them had moments of doubt at some point or other and wished they were back at home. Mostly, they just wanted to know how I was doing, and a number of the teams who had a satellite phone on board asked for my number. Consequently, as Andrew made his way through the fleet, I started to receive more and more phone calls from the other boats.

Tim and Jo of bikini-top fame soon became the crew I conversed with the most. They initially rang from *Keltec Challenger* to say how much they admired my courage. Their words meant a great deal to me after the more pessimistic lines of so many doubters. We shared a sense of humour and, every time I remembered their turning up at the start line wearing Union Jack bikini tops, it made me smile. They called every Wednesday and Sunday whenever they could get through. Each time, they would sing me a different song but only in exchange for a joke. Unfortunately, my jokes were so bad that they soon started fining me for them. The deal was that I would cook them and their partners dinner on my return, to thank them for their continued support. The catch was that every time I told a bad joke they would fine me with an unusual ingredient that I would have to include in the meal. Sort of *Ready, Steady, Cook, Keltec Challenger* style. I spent hours trying to think up jokes, but eventually had to put out a plea on the website. Within days I was being inundated with jokes from all around the world – but still, Tim and Jo didn't laugh. I had to face up to facts: it wasn't the jokes that were bad, just my delivery of them!

The same could not be said of Tim and Jo's singing – they both have great voices. I was entertained with renditions of hymns, Tom Jones numbers, and songs by Wham! and Abba. But the *pièce de résistance* was a rendition of the Jacky Wilson number 'Reet Petite'. It left me chuckling for hours afterwards. (They even called to sing me Christmas carols after they had finished and were back in England. Their dedication to my cause is something I shall never forget.)

I was grateful to all the competitors who contacted me, but occasionally had to fight back pangs of bitterness when I spoke to some of them. Why did I have to prove myself by continuing solo before they would take me seriously? Some crews who hardly gave me the time of day in Tenerife treated me completely differently in my solo state. Doubtless they were unaware of their earlier attitude to me. Initially I found my feelings hard to deal with, but I was fast developing a new relaxed outlook on life. Graced by the ocean, I found that it was not long before feelings of gratitude replaced any small amount of bitterness. After all, they were there for me when I needed them the most.

In the second week of November, the Kiwi men's team were looking set to win the race and arrive in Barbados within seven to ten days. *Challenge Yacht 24* set about heading for the finish to escort them in. Andrew switched back on to *Yacht 24* to get to dry land more quickly, but this meant we were without a phone link once again.

The days passed painfully slowly and were made worse by the continued lack of trade winds. I was not even getting close to my 30-mile-a-day target. The heat was unbearable in the middle of the day, and with no breeze the air felt sticky to inhale. Without the prospect of speaking to Andrew to look forward to, I began to feel very alone. My tower of strength was unavailable and that had a huge impact on my ability to stay focused. One afternoon I sat in the oppressive heat of the cabin, looking out through the hatch at the light glimmering off the ocean and felt as though I were trapped in a watery prison from which there was no escape.

Later that same week, during a particularly rainy night, a small bird landed on the boat. I could hear its wings flapping, but the familiar sounds of the waves took over and I assumed it had flown away. The next morning, as I cooked some breakfast, I was horrified to discover the little creature stuck in the foot well between the life raft and the bulkhead. The foot well was full of rainwater, which was lapping over its back. Only the bird's head was above the water. The poor thing had spent all night like that. I picked it up, dried it off with a towel and made it a little nest under the gunwale. The bird was so wet that it made squelching noises as it moved its wings.

Squelchy – as I quickly named him – was just the distraction I needed. So much love was building up inside me, because I hadn't spoken to Andrew, that this poor little creature was going to benefit from it, whether he wanted to or not! He became the centre of my world for the next three days. He rested well during the day, his head poking out from under the gunwale as he watched me row. But the nights were stressful. Like another Wilson's storm petrel that had visited my boat earlier in the voyage, Squelchy attempted to fly away during the early hours of the morning. I lifted him high but each time he would flap frantically from my hands, and nosedive into the sea. The dorados circled him, eyeing him up as a rare gastronomic treat. Frantic with worry that the end was nigh for my little companion, I hung over the side, splashing at the dorados and screaming at Squelchy to swim towards me. Scooped back onto the safety of the boat, Squelchy became increasingly nervous of me. He didn't realise that I was trying to help him.

By the third night I was exhausted. I had to accept that nature must take its own course. By 2 a.m. he was stretching his wings, getting ready to give it another go. I stayed in the cabin, nose pressed against the glass, sick with worry and praying that he'd make it. After a wobbly few minutes on the gunwale, Squelchy flapped over the edge and was gone. Had he become successfully airborne or was he drowning? A minute passed as I tried to shut out images of Squelchy being ripped apart by a pack of dorados. To hell with nature! I couldn't bear the mental torture any longer. I shot out of the hatch and peered over the edge into the darkness. Nothing. Squelchy was long gone. Afterwards, as I tried to sleep, I willed myself to imagine him flying happily over the ocean. I didn't want even to consider the alternative.

After Squelchy's departure my focus returned to my progress, or lack of it. It was time to face facts. The Challenge Business and *The Times* newspaper were both estimating that I would not arrive in Barbados until at least the end of January. I had set the short-term goal of reaching 30 degrees west in ten days but, as I had not even got close, a big reality check was in order. I guess I had been kidding myself for weeks that I could still make it to Barbados before Christmas. I just didn't want to accept the fact that I was likely to have to spend one-third of a year, the best part of four months, on my own in a little boat if I was to fulfil my dream. It hurt to think that I would not be with Andrew and my family at Christmas time or with my closest friends, the Wilsons and the Kings, in our Cornish cottage – already booked for New Year.

It was vital to maintain a positive attitude at this stage. After realising that I was in for a significantly longer adventure than anticipated, I worked hard each day at finding something positive to focus on. Whether that focus came in the form of a beautiful sunrise, the satisfaction of learning two more Spanish verbs or seeing some funky fish under the boat, I could generally find something. If a focus couldn't be found in my surroundings, there were always text messages to keep me going. Rowing the Atlantic alone is an excellent way to revive friendships! I heard from so many people I hadn't seen or heard from in years – one of the many unexpected highlights that my adventure produced.

Wonderfully, those messages didn't just originate from friends and family. People from all over the world sent text messages and emails encouraging me as I rowed. I even had a phone call from a complete stranger one weekend, but my most regular 'text friend' from South Africa, David G, sent me such long correspondences (each sent over several text messages) that I began to feel as if I had known him for years. He pointed out that receiving text messages from someone I was never likely to meet, while alone in a rowing boat mid-Atlantic, must be strange.

I suppose it was, but I grew accustomed to it. It was part of the charm of the experience and a wonderful way of provoking thought. In the first half of November alone I received messages from New Zealand, Australia, the USA, South Africa, an Irish pub in Germany and, of course, a huge number from the UK. Each name had a whole life behind it – family, job, hobbies, home, favourite songs, dreams and aspirations – and this was where my thoughts began. I spent endless hours rowing along and wondering what Claire from Florida looked like or what kinds of beer Robert O'Casey was serving in his pub in Einsbergh, Germany. I started to hatch a plan around finding out how right or wrong my thoughts were.

It struck me that all my text friends knew what I looked like, as they had to visit the website to send me a message. By the end of the journey they would also have a pretty good idea of my personality, my likes and dislikes and some of my history as I shared my experience in my online diary. I thought it would be great to turn the tables, uncover the lives of my text friends and find out whether I imagined them correctly. I started to daydream about what an adventure I could have, travelling around the world, visiting just one or two in each country to thank them personally for their support. I would discover how on earth they found out about my voyage in the first place, and listen as they told *their* stories. It would be fascinating. I was certain that my text friends would be as diverse as the countries they lived in. The only flaw in my plan was how I was going to fund the 'visiting-my-text-friends adventure'. I certainly wouldn't be *rowing* from country to country!

These text friends and their messages eased my loneliness enormously, but I was still desperate to hear Andrew's voice. We were still a team, whether Andrew was in the boat or not, and I knew I couldn't do it without his help and support. By now, his yacht, along with the leading Kiwi men's team, was delayed by unusual weather conditions as a result of nearby Hurricane Michelle. For me it meant further days without hearing Andrew's voice, but for Steve and Matt on *New Zealand Telecom Challenger 1* it meant a far worse disappointment. They had enjoyed a fantastic race and were set to smash the world record of 41 days, but would now narrowly miss out owing to the weather.

On 16 November, just over a month after getting off *Troika Transatlantic*, Andrew arrived in Barbados. I was so proud of him. He had sailed the Atlantic – a big achievement in its own right, particularly for someone with a fear of the ocean. I had arranged the previous day to call the Challenge Business race-control satellite phone at 10 a.m. I could hardly contain myself in the hours leading up to making the call and was leaping around the deck with Woody the bear shouting, 'We're going to speak to Vealy; we're going to speak to Vealy!'

I watched the minutes tick by and could wait no longer. I dialled the number and my heart sank as I got the voice-mail service. I hung up and sat looking at the horizon, feeling completely deflated. I suddenly realised that I should have left a message telling him to call me as soon as he picked it up, so I redialled and Andrew answered.

'It's you!' I shouted in a surprised voice.

'Of course it is,' Andrew replied. 'I was told you'd ring at this time.'

I blurted out that I had tried to call and had got the messaging service, that I'd been so excited – 'and then you didn't answer and, and, and . . .'

'It's OK baby, I'm here now.' As always, Andrew had soothed me within one sentence. Lots of telling each other how much we loved and missed each other followed – and little else. It had been only ten days since we'd spoken but it felt like a lifetime. 'I don't ever want to go that long without speaking to you again,' vowed Andrew. 'I don't, either,' I replied, feeling all loved and needed once more. Who cared if we *were* being schmaltzy – certainly not us!

Two days later Steve and Matt on *Telecom Challenger 1* crossed the finish line. They had not broken the world record, as they'd hoped, but they *had* won the Ward Evans Atlantic Rowing Challenge – I still had almost two thousand miles to go.

It was wonderful to hear all about the finish from Andrew, now safely landed in Port St Charles. It sounded fantastic and hearing about it only increased my anticipation, even though I still had months to wait. It certainly made me pull harder for a while. Andrew explained that he had been keeping himself busy attending cocktail parties, and that I was not to worry – he'd had a drink for me in my absence. Never let it be said that my husband is not a generous man!

It was the start of what was to become a complete contrast in our lifestyles. Andrew moved into the farmhouse home of the manager of Port St Charles and his wife, Thomas and Cath Herbert. Andrew's text messages at that time highlighted just how different our daily lives were becoming.

> ✉
>
> Seen Thomas's house in the daylight now. Just the 300 acres! Time to get back to my hammock and dream of you. I love you more than ever. xxx.

Adversity is such a strange thing. There I was, seemingly suspended in dark water five kilometres deep with another six hours of rowing to complete before I could rest, while Andrew, homemade rum punch in hand, lay suspended in a hammock watching monkeys swinging in the palm trees. Did I mind? Not at all. I was just relieved that he was safe and pleased to hear him sounding so happy.

With *Challenge Yacht 24* at the finish line, *Yacht 47* made its way to the back of the fleet to provide safety backup for us slower contenders. One morning after the Kiwis had finished the race, I sat at the oars, bleary-eyed at 6.30 a.m. trying to decide whether the green light I could see on the horizon was a green star or the starboard-side mast light of the Challenge yacht. As I was aware only of red planets and not green ones, I decided that it must be the yacht and busied myself tidying up – I'm a very boat-proud person, you know (women . . . typical!).

Once the tidying was complete, I felt very calm as I watched them gliding towards me. I was so content with life on *Troika* that I knew it would be a pleasure to share some time with them, but that I would not be disappointed when they sailed away.

I thoroughly enjoyed talking to them as they motored around me, having not had any human contact for five weeks. I seemed to have a surprising amount of gossip to share, which was odd considering I was mid-Atlantic and hadn't seen anyone for so long. I'm normally the last to hear everything when in the UK, but first, it seemed, at sea. I talked to the crew about the finish.

'Apparently Chay was on *This Is Your Life* as an acquaintance of Babs Powell,' I explained. 'So Alistair [another Challenge Business director] is in Barbados, presenting the prizes to the winners.'

'I can't believe you're in the middle of the ocean and you know all this stuff!' exclaimed the skipper, Lin. 'We didn't know that and we're in touch with the Challenge office!'

Consequently a rumour developed that I didn't have time to row because I was a too busy reading text messages. Thank goodness I rowed for twelve hours a day, or I fear that would have been true!

I told the crew that I was running short of writing paper and they kindly threw a pad to me in a waterproof barrel, but to my surprise I found some extra treats inside. They had enclosed a large lump of cheese and some slices of freshly baked bread. Andrew had tipped them off while he was on board that I have a bit of a thing for cheese. I was in heaven, and able to have cheese for breakfast, lunch and dinner for the next few days – cheesetastic! In return, I filled the barrel with treats for the support crew, as usually they are only givers and not receivers.

'I've put a few treats in the barrel for you,' I said. 'I'm sorry it's not much but it's a token of my gratitude for all you're doing.' I hoped they realised that my words were heartfelt. I didn't have much to give – a few packs of Extra Strong Mints, some boiled sweets and some chewing gum.

'Mints!' shouted Sian the medic, and dived into a packet. 'I've been craving mints for a week now.'

I was glad I had been able to give them something enjoyable. The crew had been at sea for such a long time and deserved far more then a few sweets. They had been away from home longer than I had, and were also heading for a Christmas away from their loved ones. I felt enormous gratitude to them for their continued backup support – especially as, on a more personal note, they always looked out for me, encouraging me all the way. I felt their support was with me always, even when they were hundreds of miles away from me

'How was Andrew when he was on board?' I asked Sian.

'He was fine. We talked through everything and he was OK with it all. He's just so proud of you.'

She went on to explain that they often sat together at the stern and talked about life at sea. I was pleased Andrew had been given the opportunity to talk through his fears with someone who understood. Sian was the friend he needed.

Although it was wonderful to see the Challenge yacht, I was not remotely tempted to give up and join them. I had wondered how it would feel to see them – and how I would react once they had sailed away. I was overjoyed to discover that I still felt happy and homely – just me, Woody the bear and my trusted *Troika*. My feelings hadn't changed: I still felt content as I waved them goodbye.

Around this time, one afternoon, I looked up and saw what I thought was a lighthouse on the horizon. It was the brilliant white sails of a yacht called **Wild Woman** en route from Tenerife to the Cayman Islands. I spoke to the skipper, a Londoner, for some time over the VHF and told him my story: that I'd started rowing at the beginning of October, that my speed was an average of 1.2 knots, and that I hoped to get to Barbados by the end of January 2002.

'Yes, my boat's made of plywood,' I acknowledged, nonchalantly. 'And, yes, I'm rowing solo.'

I could hear myself saying all of this and realised that it sounded absolutely absurd. Why would anyone do that? Life on the ocean

wave had settled for me and become normal, so I had quickly forgotten that what I was doing was actually more than a little strange.
It certainly appeared strange to the crew on *Wild Woman*.

'That's amazing. Rather you than me!' said the skipper.

'Can we give you anything? A beer or some food?'

It was a kind offer, but I didn't want to take anything. I somehow
felt I shouldn't have a drink until I had made it to Barbados. I
thought it would seem all the more special if I waited. I was kicking
myself by Christmas for turning him down!

'No, thanks,' I replied. 'That's very kind of you, but I'm carrying
everything I need.' 'Well, you've got until we reach the horizon, so if
you change your mind give me a call on the VHF.'

Their surprise at stumbling across me made me wonder whether
one day the enormity of what I was doing would hit me. I knew it
wouldn't happen until I reached dry land, but I fully expected to
catch myself saying at some point in the future, 'I can't believe I
actually rowed across the Atlantic Ocean on my own for three
months.' I imagined my grandchildren tutting and saying 'Granny!
What *were* you thinking of!'

Chapter 6

Virtual Hugs and Chicken Cup-a-Soup

Some days after Andrew arrived in Barbados, the Atlantic started sulking. 'Mean, moody and magnificent' summed it up nicely. It obviously had something to get off its chest and had a good old tantrum – something with which I could sympathise. Phenomenal winds and rain arrived in the small hours one morning, throwing *Troika* around as if she were as light as a ping-pong ball floating on the surface. Each wave smacked against the side of the cabin sending the boat up on her side, skittering along with the spray. The smacking noise sounded as though the boat was breaking up.

This continued for hours, but the interior of the cabin had become a kind of cocoon where, in my mind, nothing bad could happen. It now seems strange that I felt such security and comfort once the hatches were shut, when realistically only 6–9 millimetres of plywood separated me from the storm raging outside and the miles of deep, dark ocean below! What is even stranger is that I thrived in these ocean conditions. I felt less fear and more alive once the wind and the waves arrived. I preferred the rough ride to the flat calm nights that were so still and eerie.

The Atlantic often reminded me of the pupils I used to teach. The most challenging had a lively spirit in their eyes that I saw reflected in the ocean on days like these. I tried not to get offended when this feisty ocean attempted to tip me out of the boat. I knew I should not take it personally: it was just a game we played. The ocean would release its white horses to gallop across the tops of the waves towards me. To ride with them, I had to keep the boat stern on to the horses and receive the reward of a moment of adrenaline-pumping pleasure as the boat leaped on to their backs and was propelled at speeds of up to six knots, before slipping off again and coming to a lull in between the waves. This occurred because the boat was moving at a much slower pace than the waves. Then I'd begin the fight to straighten the boat once again before the next herd of horses arrived. If I was just a few degrees off the centre line they would gallop across the deck at me. It was a relentless, exhausting and often soggy game. I was happy to play it when the winds were from the east or northeast, reducing the miles between Barbados and me. But if the winds were against us, I took solace in a quotation sent to me by a friend. Every day its truth was underlined.

✉

'Great works are performed not by strength, but by perseverance.'
Samuel Johnson

I had been waiting weeks for the trade winds and the waves to arrive. When they finally showed up, they were relentless, but assisted me nicely in my progress towards the island of rum. Having spent too long watching my GPS speedo reading 0.7 knots, I was overjoyed to reach an all-time new record of 8.2 knots, while surging along on a particularly large wave. The speedo positively quivered with excitement!

I longed to get a photo of the walls of water appearing over the back of the cabin, and continuing to rise, but I knew a camera could not do the conditions justice. As I sat in the troughs, looking up at the mountainous waves, the sheer power of them was overwhelming. Some looked the size of houses as they raced towards me. I was transfixed.

I realised that, if the wind continued, I would finally reach the next milestone on my map – 30 degrees west – by Monday, 26 November, the start of the following week.

As I rowed I continued with my tactic of 'falling off' the back of the waves, before picking up another and surging along for a short time. This was still possible because the boat was moving much more slowly than the waves.

During this last week of November, the waves were particularly large and the sets of waves very close together. I loved their size and speed and didn't even consider the dangers. I was about to receive a rude awakening.

As I fell off the back of a wave, I looked up to straighten my course, only to notice a wall of water already upon me from behind. I was still travelling fast from the surge of the previous wave and my brain began to pick up warning messages. The wall seemed to be growing bigger and bigger. I began to feel as though I was about to be engulfed. But I knew the waves. I'd always risen up the front of a wave, surged along the top and then fallen off the back. This one would be no different, or so I thought.

As the wave started to pick her up, I felt the stern of the boat begin to rise as if in slow motion. I looked sideways, along the wave, and noticed that all 23 feet of *Troika* was poised on top of the front of the wave. Still I continued to rise up with the wave. I was willing *Troika* to get up and over it, knowing that at any moment I would be at the peak and surge along, then come to a lull behind the wave as it passed on through.

I edged upwards slowly, then came to a stop. We were suspended in air, in time, defying gravity. Within an instant, the slow-motion button had been released in favour of fast-forward. I found myself shooting back down the front face of the wave, in the direction I had just come from, completely out of control. I looked up at the speedo: 10 knots. I had to do something, fast. I knew that, if the speed of the boat overtook that of the wave, the bow would plunge into the base of the wave, which would then catch *Troika* up and flip us end over end. It was a manoeuvre I loved to do in my kayak playing in the surf, but this was not the time to be trying it in a rowing boat!

Then it hit me: I wasn't wearing my life jacket. I wasn't even clipped into the boat. Even worse, the cabin hatch was tied wide open. If we flipped, the cabin would fill with water and the boat would sink. The self-righting design of the boat relies on the cabin working as an air pocket, giving the boat buoyancy – but only when the hatch is shut tight.

I quickly thought about what I would do if I had been in my kayak and realised that I needed to surf along the wave, rather than straight down it. I stuck an oar into the face of the wave as quickly as I could and drove it to one side. The pressure exerted by the force of the water was phenomenal, but *Troika* slowly came round. I let go of the other oar and held onto the first, which was now juddering in the wave. I gripped tightly with both hands and applied the full force of my body weight.

Troika began to 'surf' as well as any board surfer in Hawaii. She carved across the wave like a pro, but at personal expense. I heard the plastic scuppers – spouts that allow water to drain from the deck overboard – on the starboard side creak under the force of the water. Then, a crack, and one of them was gone. The water gushed in through the open hole and spilled across the deck.

My adrenaline level was riding as high as the wave. The ride was fast, furious and exhilarating. As I rode the wave to its natural end, I turned and watched the back of it as it continued its journey across to the Caribbean.

Then *Troika* was still once again and all became calm. The thrashing noise had moved on with the wave and I was just left with the fizzing noise of oxygen being released from the aerated water all around me.

I sat motionless, my face aching from grinning so hard. But I had got off lightly and the seriousness of the situation suddenly sank in. I had thought I knew the wave but I was wrong. I had *heard* of rogue waves, but this had been my introduction to one. And my heart was pounding.

'That was a close one,' I whispered to *Troika*. 'Perhaps I'll just shut your hatch.'

Andrew was having an amazing time in Barbados: the laid-back attitude of the Barbadians matched his personality perfectly. He would happily have stayed longer, but was due to return to work. We had accumulated considerable debts through participating in the challenge, and, if we were to start paying them off, we needed Andrew's salary.

We had discussed his return to England frequently and I knew it was the sensible thing to do. But, as the day of his flight home arrived, I had managed to work myself into a state of nervous tension – undoubtedly induced by tiredness. We had been hundreds, even thousands, of miles apart for weeks and yet Andrew's returning to England somehow felt different. He was going to be so far away. What if anything went wrong and I needed him?

By lunchtime on that day, I was crying, and doing a very good impression of a severely distressed person. I became transfixed with the need to hear him say that he would drop everything and get on the first plane to Barbados if anything went wrong. I knew he always would, but I needed to hear him say it. Frantic, I called all the numbers I had. The Challenge Business race HQ was my best bet, but everyone was at lunch. By the time they called back, Andrew had left for the airport. I was inconsolable, and started to feel the walls of the watery prison closing in again. I just wanted to squash my face into Andrew's chest and feel his arms around me, loving and protecting me.

Twenty-four hours later I was finally able to speak to him. He was finding it hard to be back in England and had arrived at Hayley and Leigh's house in Plymouth. They have an understanding of his situation and our relationship that goes deeper than most. Andrew was well aware that it was time for him to face the music, but he needed a weekend at the sanctuary of Hayley and Leigh's place to rest and reflect first.

I can't imagine how hard it must have been for Andrew to return to friends, family and colleagues and admit that he hadn't been able to handle those days on the ocean. They had all given us both such incredible emotional, practical and financial support. Although I knew each one would understand, that didn't make facing them any easier for Andrew. We had no idea then that friends and family wouldn't be all he had to face. The media were poised to pick up on the story – and to run with it much faster and far further than we could ever have imagined.

It's rare for a journalist to give rather than take down information, but I later received a quotation from one who had heard our story and understood, as I did, Andrew's immense bravery. It seemed a poignant message for Andrew to keep in mind as he returned to face friends and colleagues who would undoubtedly ask him to explain what happened:

> ✉
> 'It is not the critics who count;
> not the man who points out where
> the strong man stumbled or where
> the doer of deeds could have done
> them better. The credit belongs to
> the man whose face is marred with
> dust and sweat and blood. At best,
> he knows the triumph of high
> achievement; if he fails, at least
> he fails while daring greatly, so
> that his place shall never be with
> those cold and timid souls who know
> neither victory nor defeat.'
> Theodore Roosevelt

Andrew had dared greatly and no one could claim otherwise. I respected that enormously.

Just before the end of November, the satellite tracking system recorded that I had been the second-fastest boat in the fleet the previous day. I thought, who needs two big strong guys in a boat when you can go faster with just one little me? I knew my success was largely due to the frontrunners being held up by Hurricane Olga while I was surfing at speeds of up to 10 knots down some whopping great waves. But I decided not to dwell on that minor detail! During the same week I achieved a record-breaking 43 nautical miles in 24 hours and achieved similar distances on all the other days that week. It felt that I was finally being rewarded for my weeks of patience. Playing in the big surf every day was awesome and I was completely in my element. I kept on thinking, surely I was born for this!

✉

The front of the fleet is being pushed back by Hurricane Olga. Now's your chance — 10 firm strokes, and you can catch them! Mr P

The big surf took me to 1 December almost before I realised it. I had been at sea for two months. Reaching December meant I was now able to say to Andrew, 'See you next month.' It was often hard being out in the Atlantic alone in October and November, knowing that I would not see Andrew, friends and family until January or possibly even February. But suddenly I had only a month and a bit to go. That was reassuring.

I called Hayley and told her that I thought the time would now fly by. December promised plenty to look forward to, and I expected this to make the time go faster. I knew Hayley had made up a Christmas parcel for me, which had been flown to Barbados and put on *Challenge Yacht 24*. They planned to bring it out to me at the start of December, while checking up on the boats at the back of the fleet. I was also hoping for a visit from Russ Corn, an old friend who was sailing across the Atlantic with his wife and some friends. And of course there would be plenty of phone calls from friends and family

over Christmas. On top of all this, I was escaping those endless
Christmas TV ads and town centres crowded with Christmas
shoppers. The over-commercialisation of Christmas was something
I knew I wouldn't miss.

But my expectations were falsely optimistic. Pinning too much
hope on an event often means we set ourselves up for disappointment – and this is exactly what I did. I was so looking forward to
seeing some friendly faces on the Challenge yacht. The meeting had
consumed my thoughts for so long that I hadn't even considered that
the yacht might not make it to me. I was bitterly disappointed when
I received a text message from the Challenge Business saying that
there was a problem with the yacht and they had been forced to turn
back. No friendly faces, no Christmas parcel. The significance of this
disappointment was to become huge.

✉

**Debra, CB#24 has lost its mast. Has
had to turn back so won't be
visiting you. T**

I had attached great importance to the arrival of the Christmas
parcel, for two reasons. First, it contained photos of Andrew
and my family and, second, meeting up with the crew of the
Challenge yacht to receive it would mean contact with other
people. The only photos I had brought on board were those of Dad
sitting on *Rio Luna*. I carried them everywhere because they
reminded me of what it really meant to fight for your dreams. I
hadn't brought photos of the rest of my family because I expected
to be away for only a short number of weeks. I didn't have any of
Andrew because I thought I would have the real McCoy sitting in
the boat with me.

A few hours later, I saw the first glimpse of another yacht mast
appear on the horizon. An hour later it was apparent that it was
heading straight towards me. I tried to contain my excitement as I
convinced myself that Russ Corn must have called the race HQ for

my latest position and was coming to visit. All was not lost. My emotions were on a roller coaster, but I was going to have some much-needed human contact after all.

I excitedly dashed into the cabin to put on some clothes, and even treated myself to a baby wet-wipe session, digging out some deodorant from the bottom of the battery compartment. As I got ready, my imagination ran through meeting-up scenarios; what we might talk about; what kind of fresh food they would be able to give me. I even went as far as imagining that I could climb aboard for a hug and share a meal and a cold beer with them.

Once dressed, and with VHF radio in hand, I waited for the yacht to get within range. It was definitely coming straight for me – it must be Russ! Then just as I was about to start calling on the radio, the yacht tacked and begun sailing towards the horizon. Maybe they hadn't seen me and were scanning the area. I'd call them. It would be OK. No problem.

'*Resolution, Resolution, Resolution*, this is *Troika, Troika, Troika*. Over.' Nothing. Maybe they were all up on deck, unable to hear the VHF below. '*Resolution, Resolution, Resolution*, this is *Troika, Troika, Troika*. Over.'

There was still no response. By the third time, I was screaming into the VHF. They were still so close. Why weren't they answering? I resorted to a more basic method of getting their attention and started frantically waving my bright red Musto waterproofs in the air, but they didn't change their course.

They were sailing away.

I had so much wanted it to be Russ that I had convinced myself that it must be. But it wasn't. It was an unknown crew on an unknown yacht, who certainly weren't looking for me, and who could never understand the downward rush of emotions the sight of them had caused.

The initial excitement of having reached December had evaporated. The loneliness I felt as I hit rock bottom was almost unbearable. Over the next ten days it engulfed me.

As a tactile person, I was missing Andrew's hugs. I hadn't realised just how much physical contact I generally had with others on a daily basis – even simply brushing past someone on the train – until I was completely alone. Normally the ocean and its inhabitants were a great source of company, but since the wind and the waves had grown bigger I had seen few signs of life. I missed the turtles and the whales. Their absence only added to my loneliness.

I had reached an all-time emotional low, which had a dramatic effect on me in every way. My body began to reject all food and water. I struggled to drink a single litre of water a day when I should have been drinking eight to ten. Consequently I felt weak, and rowing seemed harder than ever. I just couldn't fight with the waves in such a condition and constantly dissolved in tears while sitting at the oars. Every minor task seemed like a major challenge and caused even more bottom-lip trembling. I felt as if I were losing the will to live. I wanted to climb into the cabin, curl into a ball and hope that one day I would drift onto a beach in Barbados.

I forced myself to write a diary entry, but couldn't face trying to make it sound as if everything was peachy and I was having a fabulous time. I had always tried to sound positive in my diary updates, to avoid worrying my family and friends, but I didn't have the energy any more. For the first time, my diary contained the absolute truth. I shared my unbearable loneliness and told them that all *I* wanted for Christmas was a hug. The last thing I wanted was for Andrew to start blaming himself for my loneliness because I certainly didn't. *I* had chosen to go on alone and it was *my* responsibility to accept the consequences.

Somehow, writing everything down made me feel better. The self-inflicted pressure of wanting everyone to think I was doing well had become too much. I couldn't be anything other than honest. Within hours of my diary entry being posted on the *Troika Transatlantic* website, I was inundated with supportive text messages from around the globe, becoming the proud recipient of more virtual hugs than anyone else in the world!

✉

Express delivery for Mrs Debra Veal. An unfeasibly large and extremely huggy hug. With lots of love *H. Oh go on . . . have another one then!

Not surprisingly, I had more responses from that diary update than any other. My phone could hold only 30 messages, so each time I cleared the inbox, it filled up straightaway with another 30! The words were so encouraging and almost always cheered me up, but one set of text messages left me sobbing. They were not tears of sadness, but of self-revelation, and instantly had the power to wash away my loneliness. They were from Matt Jess.

✉

Really concerned about you not keeping up your fluid intake. I am on dialysis and can only drink 1 litre of fluid a day. I hate it. I constantly feel thirsty and wish to be able to have a good long drink. Kidney problems are no cup of tea. You must not put your body under extra pressure. It's not worth it. PLEASE go and drink at least 2 litres of water NOW and stop me worrying so much. If you want to know why I am so worried it's because I have been through a lot during the last 2¹/₂ years as a result of my kidneys. I don't want anyone to go though what I have, especially friends. Keep smiling and keep drinking! Matt Jess.

I immediately reached for my water bottle and began to drink. I was drinking for Matt – because he couldn't. After that, I drank every fifteen minutes by the clock. Matt had shown me the depths to which I had sunk. Not eating or drinking was only making things worse. I subsequently discovered that Matt had trained for the BT Global Challenge Around-the-World Yacht Race. He too had ocean dreams, but these were harshly taken away from him shortly before he was due to set sail in 1997, when he discovered he had the onset of kidney failure. In every message Matt had sent, I felt as if he were living his ocean dreams through my voyage, and now I understood why. I couldn't let him down. And, if I didn't drink, I would damage my own kidneys.

I realised that there are individuals like Matt all around the world, whose dreams are shattered or put on hold by illness, and countless others dying or starving in war zones and developing countries, their dreams unfulfilled. Yet there I was on a boat with food I wasn't eating, whingeing about being lonely, yet with the chance to fulfil *my* dreams – how lame!

When I returned to the text messages later, I realised that this voyage was no longer just about a girl in a rowing boat. There were so many more people involved now. Thousands were visiting the website and many hundreds were sending me text messages, sharing how my voyage was helping them. I was inspiring people to follow their own dreams, and they in turn were inspiring me to hang on to mine. I felt so humbled by this.

✉

```
I am a New Yorker rooting you on.
My students sang the Harbo &
Samuelson song and read your diary
entries. Kathy
[Harbo & Samuelson were the first
crew to row across the Atlantic,
back in 1896.]
```

✉

Hi Deb. Got a cold, feeling blue, read your diary page — inspired at last — work to do! Keep up the good work! Love Deb Ward

✉

Morning, Jo here. Weird experience today. Met someone in a meeting who I never met before. I mentioned I rowed. He said have you heard of that amazing woman who is rowing the Atlantic single-handed. That's you DV! It was wonderful to hear the impression u are making on people you have never met. L.o.l, Jo xx

✉

Had trouble bathing 2 kids last night — water everywhere. Thought of you battling Atlantic and felt very silly. Nicola U

✉

One of my pupils ended a story with the conclusion that people can't make a difference — you prove we can. Sarah Diggle

I believe that a negative situation can nearly always be turned into a positive one and, if nothing else, there is always the scope to learn. A text from my good friend Mike allowed me to see how. 'I think despair comes just before enlightenment,' he said, and he was right. When we are at our lowest ebb, our emotions raw and our resources stretched, we have the opportunity to discover ourselves. Whether we choose to take that opportunity is another matter. I was given that opportunity – and more time to explore it than most. I learned an enormous amount about myself and what I was capable of achieving. I was pushed beyond my fear threshold and out of my comfort zone so many times during the voyage, but it was only by being pushed beyond these outer limits that I discovered just how strong my mind was.

I realise now, how often I may have chosen the easy option in the past, either because I wasn't aware of my mental strength or because I feared failure. We all choose the easy option from time to time if we're honest. And when fear is paralysing – as was Andrew's fear of the sea – stepping back is the right thing to do. But, if the mind is willing and up for the challenge, the easy option may ultimately leave us unfulfilled.

As I thought through these issues, I remembered a time in my life when I had chosen the easy option and regretted it. I was spending the summer in the French Alps, climbing and kayaking with Mike, my climbing guru friend. He was a far more experienced climber, and highly qualified, so I was often aware that I was holding him back. One of the peaks we hoped to 'bag' was the Barre des Ecrins, standing at just under 3,000 metres. The walk in had been a long one, up the side of the Glacier Blanc, and had taken most of the day. My feet felt unbearably heavy as we walked the approach to the bivvy site – a rocky area off to one side of the glacier where we were going to sleep. Even at that altitude the air felt thin and my breathing had become laborious. My strides were so short by this point that I was hardly moving.

Mike was incredibly patient and encouraging, but my plummeting confidence and the doubt in my mind repeatedly told me that I couldn't make it, and that I was becoming a burden to him.

We slept just under the summit along with other groups of climbers. It was a typical summit climb. We had planned to get up at 3 a.m. and start our ascent with everyone else, reaching our goal and descending again before the sun came up and melted the snow and ice on the top. But, before we even went to sleep, I told Mike that I didn't have the strength to make it. I *thought* I didn't, but looking back I'm sure my lack of physical strength was all in my mind. At sea I had been given a second chance to learn the lesson. My voyage was teaching me that where the mind leads the body follows.

In the Alps I had chosen the easy option. As I watched the other groups ascending, roped together, ice axes in hand and little head torches bobbing up and down in the darkness, I felt enormous regret. I still have a postcard of that mountain stored in a box at home and I occasionally look at it to remind myself that the easy option is rarely the right option.

Before we left Tenerife, I had sat on the balcony watching the sunset over the sea and promised myself that, no matter what happened during the race, I would not take the easy option. Now, ten weeks later, I had been faced with that choice and had turned my back on the doubt. It was time to implement the sum of my mountain experience and choose to be strong. I still had 1,280 miles to go and I *was* going to make it.

With a bit of help from my friends, I had lifted myself from the depths of loneliness and believed that I would row all the way to Port St Charles, Barbados. I had come too far to give up now. Patience was what I needed and if I could find it I would soon know the most overwhelming sense of achievement, which would never be taken away from me. It would be an achievement that would make all the days of loneliness worth it.

I kept thinking of a quotation that was painted on the bulkhead of the Atlantic rowing boat *Bright Spark*, which had already finished in sixth place. It was the epitaph of Captain Webb, which said NOTHING GREAT IS EASY. The lonely days had been hard – harder than anything I had ever had to deal with before – but they were now behind me and vital lessons had been learned.

The following day a swordfish and a shoal of dorados returned to swim along under the hull – company at last. The swordfish enjoyed surfing down the big waves behind the boat, and as I watched it swimming off the stern, I realised that the food chain had just got longer. The dorados were under the boat trying to eat the flying fish; the swordfish was following in an attempt to eat the dorados. I just hoped that some enormous beastie wouldn't start following the swordfish, licking its lips; otherwise we might both be next in the food chain!

With the wind and the waves still dominating the scene, I made good progress at a fast rate of knots, and by the end of the first week in December had reached the halfway mark. I was already well over halfway in terms of time remaining, as the second half of the Atlantic is generally much faster – extra fast for me, as I had experienced such unfortunate weather conditions: no trade winds for the first 1,250 miles. My ship's logbook had only 60 days' worth of pages, because Andrew and I had hoped to finish in well under this time, so another notebook became logbook No. 2. I took the liberty of numbering only Days 61 to 100, as I set myself the goal of completing the challenge in less than a hundred days. Christmas Day would be Day 80 with Day 100 falling on Monday, 14 January 2002. It was going to be close.

> ✉
>
> **Another quote for u: Perpetual optimism is a force multiplier — Colin Powell. Godspeed, Adrian**

It became incredibly exciting to plot my position on the chart at this time. For so long, it had looked as if I would never get away from the coast of Africa and the Cape Verde Islands. I had made such slow progress without the trade winds that, by this point, I had resorted to plotting my position only every ten days. I was still unrolling the chart from the Africa side, but, with more ocean behind me than in front, it became a real pleasure to spread the chart across the cabin and see how far I had come.

Unfortunately, my chart was not the only thing I spread across the cabin just then. On 7 December I recorded in my logbook, 'This day shall forever be known as "Tomato Soup Disaster Day".' After hours of rowing in the rain, I was soaked and actually feeling quite cold. It was a chilled-to-the-bone type of coldness that I had often experienced during drizzly days walking on Dartmoor. I stopped, intending to have a hot drink, then stripped off my wet kit and crawled into the cabin with a mug of tomato soup. I huddled up with my back to the side wall and held the mug close to my face. The steam rising from the soup warmed me and also made my nose tingle. A few sips later, sheltered from the wind, the chilling cold began to lift from my body.

As I began to relax, I wondered whether anyone had sent me a text message. Without thinking, I placed my mug on the cushions next to me, let go and reached for the satellite phone. I was so used to the violent motion caused by the waves that I didn't even notice it. I moved with the boat. Mugs of liquid don't. Within seconds the scalding-hot soup was running all over the cushions. As the boat rolled from side to side, it spread fast, covering every inch of the cabin with a ghoulish red stain. I jumped aside as it burned my bottom and shouted at myself, 'Debra, you are such an idiot!'

I grabbed my only towel and tried to dam the path of the red river, but it was too late. The cushions held the worst of it, but it had also covered my pillow, run down the side of my clothes storage area and caught the edge of my sleeping bag. But then I noticed the horror of all horrors – Woody, the ship's bear, was lying in a large pool of red.

'Woody!' I reached out to him. 'I'm sorry, Woody.'

He felt heavy as I scooped him up. His stuffing had soaked up the soup like a sponge and left him looking like as if he'd been in a boxing bout with a bigger bear – and lost. I was so upset. I had become ridiculously attached to Woody as the journey progressed. He was my comfort, companion and partner in adventure. I was mortified.

I threw the towel over the soup-soaked area and headed out of the cabin with Woody. As if on cue, the rain stopped and the first sun of the day began to shine through the greyness. As any child will tell you, teddy bears hate having baths, but it was the only course of action. I pulled out the washing powder, filled a bucket and submerged Woody into the soapy liquid. He was not a happy bear, and bobbed up pathetically.

'I'm sorry, Woody, but it's got to be done,' I said.

The bright-red goo was ingrained in his fur and did not come out easily. The stench of tomatoes was even harder to remove. Once the worst of it was washed off, there was nothing else for it but to hang him up to dry. Having taken two clothes pegs from the cabin, and being careful not to show Woody what was coming, I lifted him up to the safety line and, wincing, pegged each ear in place. Would he ever forgive me? It's a hard enough life as a ship's bear. But poor Woody's embarrassment was not to end there. He had to endure endless taunts from the other bears via text messages:

⊠

Dear Pegs! Watch out for the soup tonight! Love George Bear

⊠

Told the boys about Woody's soup experience. They are still laughing!

By the time I reached the halfway mark, 20 out of the 35 crews who had started the race had finished, and three crews had retired, resulting in two of the boats being scuttled. All three of the retired crews had seen one team member drop out, with the second continuing solo. Jon Gornall, a journalist from *The Times*, had lasted the longest, but eventually the solitary lifestyle became too much, and he too decided to call it a day. I was the only solo rower, and the only female, left in the race.

I began to get text messages from competitors who had not only finished – like the Australian and New Zealand crews – but were back in their own countries. David, a supporter from South Africa, sent a text saying that it must be hard for me knowing that so many of the crews had finished, while I was still only halfway. But it wasn't. I loved hearing about the finishes and often called the race office in Barbados to get the juicy details from Teresa, the race manager. I felt enormously happy for every crew that reached Barbados, and shared their excitement, even though I knew I would probably be the last in. But it was still close! I often caught up with team *Kaos* – Malcolm and Ben from Scotland – and had overtaken them twice at various points in the race. At times I let myself think that perhaps I wouldn't be last after all.

> ✉
>
> I hear you are learning Spanish. You, young lady, will learn Hungarian too! First lesson: I am rowing — en evezek. It will not get you far in a restaurant but deals with the matter at hand! Istvan (UniS Voyager)

By the middle of December it became apparent that the media were interested in us. I found it all bemusing and hard to comprehend. After we were featured in the *Daily Express* and *The Times*, phone calls came in thick and fast, and dealing with the enquiries became a full-time job for Andrew. He phoned me laughing and said, 'Now life has become really surreal. It seems we will be appearing on the Richard and Judy show on Monday!'

We couldn't understand what all the fuss was about. For me it didn't seem real. Obviously I hadn't seen any of the newspaper articles and was far removed from it all. I felt the best thing I could do was concentrate on getting myself to Barbados – not being a media babe.

On Wednesday, 19 December, as I climbed out of the cabin to start a new shift, I noticed the sails of a yacht in the distance. I watched for an hour as it sailed towards me, until it became obvious that we wouldn't be missed. I dashed into the cabin to put on some clothes just as the sails started to drop, a sure sign that the crew were stopping for a chat. I was so excited to be having unexpected contact with other humans!

Seventh Heaven was skippered by a French guy called Plume. With him were Pete and Nikki, a young British couple, his crew from Gran Canaria to Barbados. When they discovered that I'd been at sea for so long, Nikki ran off to the galley to fetch me a loaf of freshly baked bread and some white chocolate biscuits. Only two hours before, I had been recording the desperate food situation in my logbook and now I had the opportunity to gorge myself on fresh bread, jam and chocolate biscuits!

Somebody up there was definitely watching over me.

It really is a small world. I have met university friends on the tops of mountains while skiing in France, shared a lift in London with an acquaintance from years back and sat in a plane next to the boss of the very person I was flying to visit! I had never met Pete and Nikki before, but we had come together in a vast space with a surface area of 106 billion square kilometres, where the chances of us being in the same one square kilometre at the same time must have been tiny.

It's not just a small world: it's a small ocean.

As they sailed away, I was kicking myself for not having taken down an email address. There's something strange about meeting people unexpectedly in the middle of an ocean. I felt as though I'd made lifelong friends even though I had met them only briefly. Yet I had no way of getting in touch with them in the future. They will never know just how grateful I was for the bread and biscuits (they tasted out of this world) and especially for sharing ten minutes of their time when my world had been so solitary.

Yachts are like buses. You wait for ages and then two come along at once. Well, in close succession, anyway. *Santa* (the Challenge Business yacht) arrived at dawn five days before Christmas, carrying my long-awaited Christmas parcel. In the pre-dawn I had watched the mast light slowly becoming brighter as they sailed towards me and couldn't decide whether I was more excited about the Christmas parcel or seeing friendly faces. I think the faces won. The crew launched a dinghy and Gavin and John, two crew members, rowed over with two big bin liners full of food and presents. I couldn't believe it! The 'Christmas parcel' that had been sent out from the UK had spent some time in the Challenge Business office in Barbados, where a number of people had added to it. There were so many goodies that I had to repack the boat to fit everything in. John and Gavin kindly hung onto the side of *Troika Transatlantic* for ten minutes so that we could have a face-to-face chat, which was wonderful. When the time came for them to row back to the yacht, I wanted to give each of them a big hug, but I guess I was a bit out of practice at socialising and felt too embarrassed.

I watched the yacht disappearing over the horizon, already feeling emotional because of everyone's kindness, when *Troika* was suddenly surrounded by dolphins. It was as if they had been sent to console me with their company. I tried to count them, as they numbered as many as thirty, but they moved too fast. Seeing them so close made two things immediately apparent: their comparatively small size and their wonderful characters. Every movement was enormously playful. They seemed to have permanent grins on their faces. As I watched, two of them leaped out of the water and completed front flips, landing with big splashes. To be an audience of one for such real-life entertainment in the wild was magical. I stood watching them with the biggest smile on my face, crying tears of happiness, feeling like the luckiest person alive. It really was the most beautiful Christmas present.

The following day was the last before Christmas leave for everyone at the Troika office in London, so I arranged to surprise them by wishing them a merry Christmas via speaker phone during their staff meeting. Only Andrew and one colleague knew what was planned, and as soon as they heard my voice they started cheering. A room full of people cheering does not travel well via satellite phone and it sounded more like thunder! But it meant so much to me. Andrew later told me that he was struggling to hold back tears of pride as he watched the faces of his colleagues.

I knew that the Christmas break meant that my 'lifeline' messages would drop off dramatically, as people were away from their computers and busy celebrating the season with their families. I had enjoyed an amazing week but was worried about tackling Christmas alone, so I put out a plea: 'If you do happen to have a PC at home I would really love to hear from you . . . bad cracker jokes; which films are on TV; who makes it to the Christmas number one spot on *Top of the Pops*; what the Queen has to say; which flavour Quality Street are left in the bottom of the tin . . . all the usual stuff.'

All I had to do was wait and see what kind of response I would get.

Hayley had enclosed some Christmas decorations for the boat in my parcel. I looked forward to putting them up, but didn't know how Christmassy I would feel. For some time, I'd been racking my brains as to what I could have for my Christmas meal, but the closest thing I had to turkey was a chicken-flavoured Cup-a-Soup. I remember thinking, how sad is that! But at least it would make an alternative Christmas to remember.

✉

Debra, How's the Xmas shopping?
Perhaps you shop at Shellfishdges,
Whaleworths, or Oilrigby & Pellar!
Keep it up! Andy Mason.

Chapter 7

Lonely Days
and Stormy Nights

As Christmas Day approached, the wind retreated and my average daily mileage took a severe nose dive as a result. The heat became unbearable as flat conditions returned for the first time since the end of November. During my rest period in the middle of the afternoon, I hid inside, attempting to stay out of the burning rays. I would squash myself into the end of the cabin, but, as the sun moved around, the rays would shine in directly through the hatch. Much as I curled myself into a ball I could not get my whole body into the shade, so inevitably my bottom was left to roast. I hoped that this was more a reflection on the tapered shape of the cabin than on the size of my bum!

At last I slid my way over the thousand-miles-to-go mark, inducing a very large smile. A thousand miles may seem like a long way still to go, but, with a total journey of just under *three* thousand, the thought of having only hundreds of miles remaining, rather than thousands, was a fantastic one. I celebrated with a pack of honey-roasted peanuts, found in my Christmas parcel, and a swig of purified seawater (no one had had the forethought to include a bottle of wine or can of beer!). I called Andrew to share my good news. He had just arrived at Joanna and Pete's house. They had kicked off their

Christmas celebrations with Scottish smoked salmon and champagne. Sometimes life just isn't fair!

On Christmas Eve the wind started to build from the south, dropping my rowing speed to 0.5 knots. It took me two hours to row one nautical mile, by which time the wind had swung round to a southwesterly headwind and I lost the mile I had just worked so hard to gain. It was back to playing *that* demoralising game again. I realised I was in for a long Christmas if the game continued.

A weather report from John Searson confirmed the worst – headwinds until Boxing Day. So the para-anchor went out and I settled in for a relaxing Christmas without any rowing. I had been wondering whether to take Christmas Day off, and now the decision had been made for me. Luckily I had plenty of books to read, thanks to the crew on *Challenge Yacht 47*, and had the Christmas decorations to put up. The tinsel was *Troika* blue.

Andrew headed off to his brother's house for a family Christmas, the first he had spent with his own family in five years. I called to inform him of the headwinds and expressed my concern about drifting back over the thousand-miles-to-go mark. Ever the optimist, Andrew reassured me, 'Well, if you do, at least you'll have the pleasure of reaching that milestone all over again.' Hmm!

Later that night, a further round of text messages from Matt Jess put everything into perspective once again. The text messages had dropped off dramatically over Christmas, but Matt had still managed to find the time. This message was sent over several texts:

⊠

```
Just got back in from dialysis so
thought I would drop you a line.
Not much news here. Robbie Williams
got Xmas no 1 with redo of Sinatra
song. Old guy I knew from dialysis
got transplant tonight. Possibly 2
will be done tomorrow. Really happy
for him (& them hopefully) but a
```

bit wistful as well. Inevitably
wish it was me. Having a quiet Xmas
at home. Part of me will be on a
little rowing boat in Atlantic. It
will be hard, but do try and enjoy
the day. Never be another like it.
There will be so many of us
thinking of you that you will in no
way be on your own. Take care and
happy Xmas. Matt Jess.

Christmas Day was wonderful, largely due to the forethought of Hayley. What would I do without her? While organising my Christmas parcel at the beginning of November, she had sent out a circular email asking people if they would like to send me Christmas cards to include. The response was unbelievable. She explained that, the day after the email went out, so many cards arrived for me that the postman had had to ring the doorbell in order to deliver them. It took me two hours on Christmas morning to open and read them all. They were a joy and really made my Christmas.

Other great presents included an excellent Santa hat, *The Blue Day Book*, and a beautiful necklace from Andrew – a small stone pendant carved into the shape of a turtle. My brother Matt sent me a turtle-shaped mood ring, a small Christmas pudding and the words to 'My Favourite Things' from *The Sound of Music*, as I would miss it on TV. (He has a warped sense of humour.) He also sent me the Spanish translation for English swear words, just in case I had mastered my eight-CD Spanish course and was in need of some fresh verbs to learn – typical of Matt! I was crying with laughter as I read through his long Christmas letter.

It was a great start to Christmas Day. A phone call from my mum and brothers soon followed – all in Devon together. It was reassuring to hear that the boys were with Mum. I worry about her being on her own now Dad has moved on. Relieved to discover that speaking to my family had not made me hopelessly homesick, I tentatively called

Andrew. I was doing well, but didn't know whether hearing his voice would cause me to wish away what I had out here. He sounded really happy and had been busy playing with his godson and my goddaughter, Stuart and Sarah. He told me he had stayed up late with his brother Richard, surrounded by instruction papers, trying to build Stuart's Christmas present – a rather large ride-on toy tractor. I was relieved to hear him sounding happy and busy with the children. It somehow made me stronger. Had he sounded sad and full of tales of how awful Christmas was without me, I probably would have dissolved into tears.

Hayley and Leigh had travelled to Scotland for Christmas to stay with close friends who had recently moved to a house on the edge of a loch. They were having the picture-perfect Christmas. It had been snowing heavily for a few days, which added to their fun. They delightedly told me about Glen and Grouch, two huge but friendly stags that came to the front door every day to be hand-fed potatoes and vegetable peelings. Hayley also sounded happy.

'I'm standing by the window and Grouch is outside with his nose pressed up to the glass,' she said. 'Bless him, I think he's waiting for us to go out and feed him. His antlers are all covered in snow and he's steaming up the window with his breath. How cool is that?'

✉

Glen and Grouch the Stags send their love and Christmas Greetings! Loveage, LB & HB x

Our situations could not have been more different. Hayley was by water, hers frozen enough to walk on, while mine was as warm as a bath. I sat talking to her in a bikini, but she was wearing multiple layers – and Leigh was busy stoking the log fire. Friends, fine food and wine surrounded her. It didn't upset me. I had got used to having a life that seemed a million miles away from those I love. But our conversations did underline how much my voyage contrasted with the lives of my family and how exceptional these contrasts were.

My mother had also been bobbing about on a boat just before Christmas, but our respective ocean-going vessels could not have been more different. As I rowed away from the Cape Verde Islands my mother had approached them, on her way from England to Cape Town, in very different style – the *QE2*. I often thought of all the fantastic food she was enjoying and the comfortable bed she was sleeping in. Dressing for dinner, white linen tablecloths and heavy silver cutlery seemed a far cry from my solitary naked dining on yet another boil-in-the-bag meal eaten with my favourite orange plastic spoon. My brother, his tongue firmly in cheek as usual, was quick to point out that my mother's luxurious ocean passage had cost a mere fraction of what it cost me to take to sea. Had she got a better deal? I guess that's a matter of opinion.

It was now Andrew's life that contrasted most with my own, and the life he had known for his two weeks on board. He had gone from the wide-open expanse of the ocean back to his job in central London. The day I had realised how wide the gap between our two worlds had become was the day I had been told that *Challenge Yacht 24* had turned back with my Christmas parcel – the day my loneliness had really set in.

Andrew had lunched at the Park Lane Hilton, at a corporate function, where he enjoyed a five-course meal, with carefully selected wines designed to bring out the flavours of the food, while my purified seawater had done nothing to hide the foul taste of the noodles and stale biscuits I was lunching on! Andrew sat down with five hundred people, when I would have enjoyed the company of one. After lunch, as I returned to the oars, he had listened to the witty talk of two speakers. I could talk only to myself.

Christmas Day had started all stormy with headwinds, but by mid-afternoon it had cleared and the winds had dramatically changed direction. I rowed through the afternoon in bright sunshine, wearing a bikini and a Santa hat, singing, 'Raindrops on roses and whiskers on kittens . . .' – words courtesy of my brother. Beat that for an original way to spend Christmas Day!

✉

No longer capable of organising Christmas without my wife! Come home soooooon!! Loveage, Andrew xxx

I later discovered that Andrew's annual prayer at the Christmas Morning church service was for me. He prayed that the headwinds I was struggling with would dissipate and the tailwinds return. The tailwinds did return, just long enough for me to have a positive, productive and enjoyable Christmas. Matt Jess was right. There would never be another like it. As I ate my Christmas pudding while watching the sun set, I couldn't help thinking that if you had to spend Christmas day alone, this was a pretty good way to do it.

The headwinds returned on Boxing Day. The para-anchor was out again and I slowly drifted backwards. I had made little progress in the previous five days and was aware that this would impact on my arrival date in Barbados. I tried not to think about the possibility that the trade winds wouldn't return in the near future and knew that I must continue to focus on maintaining a positive attitude, but as 2002 drew near it was becoming very hard. In the period between Christmas and New Year, extreme loneliness returned. I missed everyone dreadfully and just wanted to go home. Then I did something I promised myself I would never do. I started to do a mental calculation, based on my current speed, of how much longer it was likely to take me to get to dry land. The figure after the equals sign represented the best part of a month. Another whole month alone, surrounded by dark scary water. But the calculation was done and could not be forgotten. Instead of taking one day at a time, as I had done previously, I focused on the month as a whole. It seemed an impossibly long period of time. I felt as if the real challenge was, only now, about to begin.

As I approached the three-months-at-sea mark, I realised that the challenge was slowly wearing me down. Week after week of twelve-hours-a-day, solitary, hard labour was taking its toll. My body was screaming for some normality: a rest from rowing, a still bed and a toilet with a seat, regular showers and some fresh food – the things most of us take for granted. Yet I didn't want to wish away what I had out there. It was an extraordinary experience, shared by only a few. Deep down I knew I was truly lucky. I just had to remind myself of that during the tough times. My emotions were taking another roller-coaster ride. One hour I was desperate for it all to be over, the next I was content, not wanting it to end. I had to reach Barbados before the lows started to outnumber the highs – and soon.

The only way that was going to happen was if I spent more time at the oars. I had started to drop to ten hours' rowing a day and sometimes managed only eight, when Hayley sent me a message:

✉

Here's the deal — we've given you your presents. Now you have to give us ours . . . You in Barbados ASAP. I mean, no dilly-dallying and reading books when you should be rowing. We want a full 12 hours a day Mrs. Veal!

My brother Matt then followed up with:

✉

Debs — Matt here. Don't listen to Hayley — row slower. The air fares get cheaper in February!

To keep my promise to Hayley (and ignoring Matt's humour), I had stern words with myself and started a full twelve hours a day at the oars, storms permitting. I even started adding an extra fifteen minutes to my rowing shifts here and there, if I could manage it. I was on an absolute mission to get to dry land. There's only so long a girl can spend on her own crossing the Atlantic – and I wanted to finish before I started to resent that beautiful ocean.

The New Year arrived in a stormy fashion and the midnight moment turned out to be a soggy one. I dashed out of the cabin to take a photo of the GPS screen, only to be soaked by a big wave breaking against the side of the boat. Trying not to drip on the camera, I took a photo at 00.00.23, capturing the exact location where I could be found right at the start of New Year's Day 2002.

I had held this romantic idea that I would see in the New Year sitting under the full moon, watching shooting stars and savouring the utter peace and tranquillity of the ocean. This was Plan B. For Plan A, I would have been in Cornwall with Andrew and four close friends on a previously arranged New Year holiday. We had joked about the possibility of our not making it back in time to join them. At that point the idea of still being at sea after three months had seemed ludicrous.

But, without me, Andrew and our friends ate roast beef and drank copious amounts of red wine in front of an open fire, as I saw in the New Year by treating myself to half a packet of fig rolls, and toasted my absent friends with a swig of purified seawater. Another merry contrast! The fig rolls were not to be scorned, and were sadly my last. They were the most exotic food I had on board, saved for just such an occasion. New Year's Eve Plan B – full moon, stargazing and tranquillity – was scuppered by strong winds and ten-foot waves. The thick cloud cover didn't help much, either.

The remainder of that first night of the New Year was spent bracing myself against the two side walls of the cabin, in an attempt to avoid injury. The boat was thrown in all directions by the surrounding waves, and the gusting winds and rain of passing black squalls. My New Year certainly wasn't uneventful or predictable. It was, however, marred by communication problems. The idea of staying in a remote cottage is marvellous, as long as you don't want to receive any phone calls. With no landline phone and no reception on his mobile, Andrew was completely uncontactable. He could get reception on his mobile long enough for me to phone only if he walked to a certain bend in the lane leading to the cottage. Feeling very lonely, I left tearful messages on his voice mail asking him to be at the bend in the lane at a certain time. But often he didn't pick them up until it was too late. He felt helpless listening to those messages. We were both unhappy with the situation, and I wanted more than anything to be with Andrew and my friends. Not even being able to call them made it so much worse. Andrew had expressed his sentiments in a diary entry early in the New Year:

Andrew's diary update

For me, Christmas Day was the first I have spent with my family in 5 years (we normally go to Debra's family) so in many ways it was very nice. For Debra, to be sitting alone in her boat, knowing that everyone else was having Christmas and not even getting anywhere was very hard to bear. And when the twice-(or more) -daily phone calls are filled with tears and frustration, it becomes a lot harder at home.

And then New Year, we had arranged to spend with two sets of friends in Cornwall. There's nothing like going away with two couples to make you notice that, temporarily, you're not one! More frustrating by far, though, the lovely secluded house we had booked proved to be secluded from all forms of telephone communication – the first time since the yacht took me to Barbados that Debra couldn't call me at any time. The frustration of having to arrange fixed times to take calls, which inevitably didn't work out quite as planned, again made it much harder than it has been before. Many thanks to the Kings and the

Wilsons for looking after me and putting
up with my 'I miss Debra' moods!

✉

**So what are your New Year's
resolutions? Do more sport, travel
and get out more? Hee hee hee.
Charlie Kemp.**

The strong winds and mountainous waves continued throughout
New Year's Day, confining me to the cabin. The trade winds were
back with vengeance and I was on my way again. Their return
resulted in one of the greatest daily mileages of the voyage – more
than forty nautical miles – so I could hardly complain. I was not at
all surprised. I had to hang on for dear life while the waves shoved
me along at a fearsome rate. But as long as that shoving continued to
be towards Barbados I was fine. It made no difference that it was a
new year. It was just another day on the ocean wave.

✉

**U R really zoomin' Debs! Relieved 2
C your path straight 4 Barbados.
It's like the Wacky Races and U R
Penelope Pitstop. x Soph**

Being so violently 'shoved' during the nights, particularly when there
was no moon, was different. I had not realised before leaving dry
land just how often the moon is up during the daylight hours, and
not around to fulfil its night-time duties. When the moon was full at
night I could see as clearly as if it were daylight, but with no moon,
and with clouds covering the stars, I could see nothing.

The blackness cloaked everything, and was completely dis-
orientating. There was no distinction between the water, the horizon
and the sky. I could have been gliding through the air for all I knew.
I quite expected to see Mary Poppins and the children floating

through the sky off my port bow, umbrellas held neatly aloft!

I was often terrified at night. My unease with the dark, and 'loss' of sight, meant that my hearing, heightened to compensate, tended to play tricks on me. Each breaking wave sounded ominous, driving my imagination to places it did not want to go. Sometimes I imagined that the 'whooshing' sound of the waves was a whale spouting air and water through its blowhole. I would convince myself that it was getting closer and that next time it would come up directly under the boat, shattering it into a thousand pieces. Then I would imagine how it would feel to be in the black water, with creatures from the deep brushing against me, attracting other con- siderably larger creatures with considerably sharper teeth.

Yet my mind never tricked me into believing I would die. I always imagined that I would survive being in the water and would be rescued. Consequently, I didn't worry about dying, or about the boat sinking. I believed I would get through, whatever.

I guess it was this faith and self-belief that gave me the confidence to carry on alone in such an extreme environment. I also had great faith in the boat, and its design, but was realistic enough to know that it could be damaged by external objects: by ships, or half-submerged cargo containers. Mostly I tried not to think negatively, but occasionally made myself visualise an action plan for various emergency situations. I knew it was important to be prepared. 'Prior planning prevents poor performance' – as my friends in the Royal Marines had taught me.

Not every emergency situation could be planned for, however. Two stormy nights in the New Year brought situations that I had not visualised, and I was unprepared for them. Conditions became rougher the nearer I got to the Caribbean. One night, with approximately two weeks left to go, the boat was being tossed around so much that objects were flying out of the storage pockets and hitting me as I tried to sleep. I was dozing when I heard a sound that I had not heard before. The waves and the wind were familiar after I'd heard nothing else for months, but any slight variation in sound would wake me in an instant. Now, a loud cracking noise was coming from the hull of the boat.

My heart racing, I peered through the water-splashed glass of the hatch, searching in the dark for the cause. My eyes immediately focused on the port-side oar. It was still in its gate, but instead of being in the usual horizontal storage position behind the frame on the inside of the bow it was sticking, handle up, vertically into the air.

The boat had turned sideways onto the waves that were hitting the starboard side and their force had pushed the port side into the base of the wave, leaving the handle of the oar sticking up. The oar was about to snap, but the creaking noise from the pressure being exerted on the plywood hull was far more of a concern. I had spare oars, but I couldn't magic up a spare hull. The huge waves that forced *Troika* onto her side tended to come along once in every set, so there was no time to lose. If I didn't get the oar out from under the hull before the next big wave arrived, I could lose an oar and have a hole in the hull to deal with. The prospect of sinking in these conditions was not a happy one. One big wave, and I would be in serious trouble. Timewise, I felt I couldn't afford to struggle into my lifejacket and harness. I had to risk not being clipped onto the boat and hope that a 'big one' wouldn't hit while I was out on deck.

Once outside, I made a dash for the oar, concentrating on keeping my centre of gravity low to absorb the force of the waves that were breaking up against the starboard side. I didn't even notice the waves soaking me as I pulled down on the handle end of the oar in an attempt to lever the blade end from under the hull. But the weight of the boat being pushed over the oar was too much and the blade was flat against the side. The resistance was too great. I knew I would have to twist the oar so that I could feather it out of the water. I didn't stand a chance otherwise.

I leaned over the side, trying to focus on the oar rather than the mass of white foam that was splashing up into my face. I felt fearless as I thrust my arm into the cold water. Beasties from the deep were not a problem while I was still on board, but if I didn't get the oar out from under the hull I might soon be joining them. I was so focused on the task that I wasn't even scared of having parts of my body submerged in the blackness of the water.

At last, in between waves, the oar twisted. The blade cut through the water as easily as a hot knife through butter. But it was clear for only an instant, before it was ripped out of my hands and forced back into the water. As I became wetter, I began to lose my grip. Without my harness, I could have so easily have slipped over the side. In my head I was saying, 'Just stay calm, Debs. You can do this. Just one more time and you'll soon be back in the cabin.'

With the same manoeuvre repeated, I was faster at storing the handle behind the frame the second time, and had it tied up like lightning. I checked that the other oar was still secure and looked towards the hatch. It suddenly seemed a long way away. I glanced to starboard at the barrage of oncoming waves. The white water bubbling at the crest of each wave glowed in the moonlight, highlighting the mighty power of the ocean. I waited for a smaller wave, then made my move. Keeping low, I gripped on tightly to the jackstays and started crawling along the deck. The wind howled, echoing in my ears, and tossed my now dripping hair around wildly. It stuck to my face, covering my eyes and obscuring my view. I knew the jackstays led all the way to the hatch, so I just kept gripping my way across.

Back in the cabin, I felt completely unfazed by the experience. There had been a problem, it was dealt with and I would learn from the experience. It was only then that I realised how foolish I had been to be out on deck in such conditions without a harness. The consequences of being washed overboard were far worse than having a crack in the hull. The boat was being pushed along by the waves at up to four knots, so I certainly would not have been able to swim fast enough to reach the boat. Even if I had made it through the night, no one would have known that I was in the water and eventually I would have drowned. What was I thinking? My fearlessness and familiarity when working with the elements had again blurred the edges of my own limitations and concern for personal safety. Having no fear had made me a danger to myself.

The following week, when I had yet another night-time incident, I at least had the sense to consult Andrew. A mammoth wave hit me in the early hours, one morning. It tipped the boat up on its side and threw me hard against the port-side cabin wall. Not surprisingly, this instantly woke me up, but it was the complete pitch-blackness that brought me to my senses in an instant and filled me with dread. *Troika Transatlantic* was never dark because it had a whopper of a navigation light, which was mounted high on a mast on the bow.

The pitch-blackness could mean only one thing: the wave had taken out the navigation light. Not good when you're floating in the main shipping lane between North and South America. The navigation light was the only thing to prevent container ships and tankers from running me down.

As I started to consider my options, none of them looked too good. Climbing up a mast to try to fix a light in the dark with no torch, in a storm that could easily have washed me overboard, was not top of my list. Unable to decide what to do next, I called Andrew at what must have been after three o'clock in the morning. Thank goodness for satellite phones and supportive husbands. Andrew was as logical as ever as we discussed the options. We talked about setting off the emergency strobe light, as he felt it was better to be seen than risk being run down by a ship, but I was concerned that passing ships would attempt to rescue me, as they should if they see an emergency strobe. We settled on using the strobe, but I spent the rest of the night looking out for ships coming to rescue me, in between trying to sleep. Sleep was a lot less likely than a rescue. When the strobe is activated, you might as well be resting your head on the roof of a police car with its lights blazing!

When I next spoke to Andrew (at a more civilised time of the day), he was staggered, as so many times before, by the almost telepathic ability of identical twins: Hayley had phoned him first thing that morning, having had a nightmare. She knew something had gone wrong on the boat during the night, had sensed my fear and was upset and concerned. She was right about the fear. For the first time

I had experienced something of what it must have been like on board for Andrew – and it wasn't a pleasant sensation. An unnerving, niggling discomfort had stayed with me until dawn and threatened my self-belief. Andrew, however, was able to reassure Hayley that, although there had been a minor emergency, I was safe and the boat was fine.

Andrew's diary update

Both Hayley and I are getting more edgy
the nearer Debra gets to the end.
Anything that looks as if it might
threaten her achievement at the last,
after all the emotion, is hard to bear.
Hayley phoned me one morning last week,
having had a nightmare about Debra (twins
do that). Fortunately, Debra was all
right, but had just that morning called
me to say that she had had the roughest
night yet and even she had been scared.

Incidents like these did nothing for my already dwindling emotional reserves. Life on board became increasingly uncomfortable. The food situation had grown particularly desperate. At one stage I had looked forward to mealtimes, but by this point those days were long gone. It wasn't that I didn't have *enough* food to eat – I had plenty – but I had plenty of the *same* food. And therein lay my predicament.

When Andrew had been on board, we had planned to complete the race in five to six weeks. Therefore, each of the four foil-packed recipes making up our main meals would have had to be consumed only a small number of times, even though we were carrying enough to cover us for 120 days. But alone, and by the third month of eating those four meals repeatedly, I had grown to hate three out of the four with a passion and hoped, and still hope, never to have to eat those meals again – ever. I had to endure beef stew and dumplings more often as we had been donated large quantities. Initially, I quite liked it, but by the third month, the smell of its sickly syrupy sauce made me feel queasy.

Each morning I opened my new daypack, desperately hoping that it would not be another night of beef stew and dumplings. Five nights in a row was the worst I had to endure, only to open my daypack on the sixth day to a new variation: golden vegetables and dumplings. This taste exactly the same as beef stew and dumplings but without the beef. Frankly, I could find nothing golden about it. The third recipe was vegetable curry, from which the vegetables had been curried away, and the saving grace of mealtimes was chilli con carne. I perfected the art of taking a mouthful of food and swilling it down with water before I felt the syrupy texture on my tongue or tasted the all too familiar flavour. It was probably the only way to avoid starvation.

Life became even more uncomfortable when I ran out of toilet paper and had to resort to using a sock. This may not sound like a major problem, but for some reason I took it really badly. Trying to wash the sock out each time was a deeply unpleasant task and, like mealtimes, was another part of the day I loathed.

Being thrown around all day by persistent force-six to force-seven conditions did nothing for my sense of humour. As I climbed out of the cabin to begin a new shift, a wave would often wash in through the gap at the bottom of the hatch and soak the cabin. My bed, belongings and, if it was a particularly powerful wave, even the photos on the wall would take a soaking.

The nineteenth of January was a bad day. I lay on a sodden bed, under a wet cover, with my head on a wet pillow. I had been constantly thrown against the walls of the cabin by a never-ending barrage of twenty-foot waves and felt that I had been in the same situation one time too many. I wanted it over then and there but still had over a week to go. I wanted more than anything to be in a warm dry bed, curled up with Andrew, safe from the raging storm going on around me. I wanted to stop having to be brave and bold and living in a life-or-death situation. I suppose what I *really* wanted was to stop having to take care of myself.

I longed for someone else to do it for me.

Lack of sleep during those rough nights meant I overreacted to almost everything. My ability to cope seemed to dissolve. Every day felt like a lifetime. My highs were staying around for shorter periods while my lows were lingering, and that wasn't good. I'd had such an amazing adventure and I didn't want it to end negatively, but I needed to find that something extra within me.

I kept reminding myself of something that Tim from *Keltec Challenger* had said to me on the phone, after he had returned to England: 'Enjoy every last moment because the memories fade so very quickly.' I knew that the bad memories would fade the moment my little brown toes touched down on the Barbados quayside, but hoped the happy ones would stay with me for ever. I often wonder why we have the ability to forget the bad times, leaving only happy memories of an event in the forefront of our mind. Hope, perhaps? Some kind of grace?

I witnessed this ability every day in the messages I received from rowers who had already finished and were back home. Many said that they were envious of my still being out there and wished they were back at sea. I knew that the likely reality was that when they *had* been out there – as I still was – they probably couldn't wait for it to be over.

I'd done it myself. My first organised adventure was as a fourteen-year old, taking part in the Ten Tors expedition on Dartmoor. Each team is allocated ten tors (a group of rocks on the top of a hill), which they must visit in a set order over two days.

I completed the bronze 35-mile route, with badly blistered feet and covered in ticks. I said that I hated the pain, and that I would never put myself through it again. Only a year later, I had signed up for the silver 45-mile route and couldn't wait to go back for more. I wasn't the first to think that way, and I'm sure I won't be the last – it's the nature of challenge.

Chapter 8

Heading Back to the Real World

Some nights in my final week, the sky was at bursting point with stars. I knew I would not see starry skies like them back in urban England. The sunrise each morning was as soothing as ever. In my often fragile state, I needed its touch. It filled me with an overwhelming feeling of contentment. I hoped and prayed that something of that contentment would stay with me as I returned to the real world.

It increasingly looked as if my return to that real world was going to be a hectic one. I had been told to expect a number of journalists, photographers and film crews when I arrived in Barbados, and was more than a bit concerned about the transition from total isolation to a hive of social activity and media interest. Every time I thought about it, I reminded myself of part of a quotation I was sent: 'No matter what happens, never act out of character.'

Not every day was marked by fragility and concern for what lay ahead. As I got nearer to the coast, I started to see more wildlife again. One evening, I was on the phone to Andrew, tucked down by the cabin out of the wind, when, mid-sentence and without thinking of the impact on Andrew, I suddenly shouted,

'*Shark!*'

I jumped up quickly to get a better look as it swam under the boat, more excited than scared. Unfortunately for Andrew, this brought the mouthpiece of my phone directly in line with the force-six wind. He was most distressed when he was blasted with the thrashing noise of the wind, as he thought I had been eaten! We ended up having a long conversation to calm ourselves.

Looking at the pictures in my fish reference book, I learned that it was a tiger shark. I thought it was quite big at a length of about six feet, but when I read the description I was horrified to discover that tiger sharks can grow to 24 feet – another creature longer than *Troika*. I was even more alarmed to read on and discover that great white sharks often attack boats and eat sea turtles for supper. 'Swim Barney, Swim!' I shouted as I read!

Two new birds also arrived on the scene. The first was a Persil-white bird with a bright orange beak and one long pointed tail feather. I was rather excited when I first saw it because it looked so exotic that I assumed it must be a Caribbean seagull, sent to prove I was getting close. The other bird couldn't have been more different. When the Challenge yacht came out to see me before Christmas, one of the crew had asked me if I had seen birds that look like pterodactyls. It was a good way of describing them. These enormous jet-black creatures have a blood-red splash under their beaks, and are without doubt the most sinister-looking birds I have ever seen. They reminded me of the baddies in a Christmas pantomime, their wings in a V shape like the exaggerated pointy eyebrows of the biggest baddy of them all. I felt like shouting '*Boooo*' and '*Hissss*' whenever I saw one, particularly when they swooped from a great height, plucking an unsuspecting flying fish out of the air.

Reaching Day 100 felt like a huge achievement. I had known for weeks that I wasn't going to make Barbados in less than a hundred days and accepted that, hard as I might try, I could not change the weather. I had to travel at whatever speed the elements dictated. Reaching Day 100 gave me a perfect time to reflect. To mark that special day, I wanted to summarise the highs and the lows, the weird and the wonderful of one hundred days in my waterworld. I spent an enjoyable and enlightening weekend reading back through my diary and logbook to compile a series of 'Top Tens' of my voyage to include on the website. The strongest impression, as I turned the pages, was just how far I had come, not only in nautical miles, but also mentally, emotionally and spiritually. Being alone at sea had made me learn and grow in ways that might not have been possible had Andrew stayed on board. Perhaps, reluctantly, I had to believe that, for that reason alone, my solo voyage was meant to be.

Top 10 things I'm most looking forward to

10. Never eating beef stew and dumplings again.

9. Feeling and looking feminine once more.

8. Being able to sit or lie completely still (although, as Andrew pointed out, I never did before I left, so I don't suppose I'll start now!).

7. Going somewhere with snow, putting on big chunky clothes and diving into it.

6. Going home to everyone and everything that's familiar and lovely.

5. Sleeping on soft linen sheets (not a salt crystal or fish scale in sight).

4. Eating endless amounts of fresh vegetables, fruit and cheese.

3. Waking up in the middle of the night to find Andrew lying next to me.

2. Having a long, cold drink of anything other than purified seawater.

1. Rowing into Port St Charles and making the dream a reality – hugging each of my family members, with an especially large one for the world's most special husband.

During my last week at sea, navigation became all-encompassing (no pun intended!). My target – Barbados – was only about sixteen miles long, which seemed unreasonably small after I'd crossed a space nearly three thousand miles wide. Unlike stronger, double-handed crews, I didn't have the luxury of being able to challenge unhelpful wind directions. I pretty much had to go in whichever direction the wind took me. Luckily, it initially headed in a strong southwesterly direction towards Barbados, but as I got closer it started to push me further south than I would have liked. I was in danger of dropping below the island or missing it altogether.

This was not a problem from the point of view of my finish line, as we had been disqualified from the race and therefore my finish line was no longer the breakwater at Port St Charles. The race had to be completed unaided, so when we received outside assistance from the support yacht who picked up Andrew we were disqualified. It didn't bother me. I was determined to win the race before we left Tenerife but, looking back, I realise that ambition had left me on the first night, when I'd first glimpsed Andrew's fear. By Day Two I knew the experience was going to be vastly different from the one we had set out to have. The race no longer mattered. Our sole focus became getting across the Atlantic – together. We really wanted to have the time alone and to have our big adventure. Winning and proving all my doubters wrong no longer mattered.

I later wondered whether it ever really mattered. It taught me how important Andrew is to my life and gave me a sense of perspective that had been sorely lacking. I could still row an ocean, something very few women had done, but it ceased being about records or marking my place in history. It became 100 per cent about the journey and what I leaned and experienced along the way.

So my finish line became just a line of longitude – 59°37′W. On crossing it I could officially be classed as an ocean rower. This line extends above and below Barbados, so it didn't really matter where I crossed it. But Port St Charles is towards the northern end of Barbados, so I knew that, if I did drop below the island to cross the line, I would almost certainly be unable to row in to where my friends and family would be waiting. The uncooperative winds meant that my only option would probably be a tow from the Challenge yacht up the leeward side of the island to Port St Charles.

I didn't want to be towed, having come so far under my own steam. So I started to focus hard on both the rowing and the tactics for staying north of Barbados. Andrew and Pete had been tracking every mile from England and were helping me bring *Troika* in. When the winds were more directly from the east, I rowed with all my might to gain the few miles back to the north that I had lost earlier in the week. Deciding how many miles to gain northwards while I had the opportunity was a real dilemma. If I went too far north when I crossed 59°37'W, I would be pushed past Barbados and it would be 'St Lucia, here I come!' and I would still need a tow from the Challenge yacht.

I was closer than ever to my trusted companion *Troika* during the closing stages. I thoroughly understood how to handle her, and she seemed to understand me. I had lived and breathed with that little boat for over a hundred days. We knew each other well. I made use of that knowledge in my rest periods and when I was sleeping at night, by offsetting the rudder and distributing the weight to different sides of the boat depending on which direction I wanted to drift in. This included my having to remember not to roll to the other side of the cabin while I was asleep, so that I didn't neutralise the beneficial effects with my body weight.

Meanwhile, Andrew kept a close eye on the other remaining team, the guys in *Kaos*. They were approximately two days in front of me and Andrew wanted to see how the weather conditions affected their approach to the island. I hoped to be able to learn from them.

I was to be the last boat in.

My final consideration was making sure that I arrived on the right day, as my family and Sir Chay Blyth were not able to fly out until Friday, 25 January. If I went too fast during the final week, they would miss my finish; but, if I slowed down and then got caught up in unhelpful weather, I would either end up drifting south below the island or get driven backwards. If the head winds returned, I could be delayed by days, even weeks, meaning that some of my family would have to fly home again without celebrating my arrival. A depressing thought. The media added their own pressure by wanting me to arrive in daylight hours. I was keen to please everyone, but ultimately knew I was at the mercy of the weather. I could take only one day at a time.

✉

Debra — Have a spare place for dinner. Are you busy? CBxx

With just a few days to go, my mood lifted and I found it hard to contain my excitement. It started to feel real – I was really going to make it after all that time! I planned to finish on the Saturday, 26 January, so Andrew flew out to Barbados on the previous Wednesday. He was due to pass overhead at about three in the afternoon. I thought it would be brilliant to wave madly skywards and yell, 'See you later!' But thick cloud cover meant I couldn't see or hear the plane on its approach to the island. It didn't matter. I knew I was going to be with him in a matter of days, and just having him back in Barbados, now so close, felt comforting.

Seeing planes overhead was a big deal. I had seen nothing but sea and sky for so long that spotting signs of 'civilisation' was exciting, but also daunting, producing a real jumble of emotions. While I was eagerly anticipating signs of land – insects and all the other things that appear only around a landmass – I knew there would be negative signs too. Pollution and artificial light would ruin my ability to see the wondrous starry skies at night – an experience I had delighted in. The ocean had been a breathtakingly pure place to live. The air was so clean that I hadn't washed for weeks and yet my skin had never been so healthy and my pores so clear. I would miss the clean living and endless amounts of fresh air.

I suppose in many ways the ocean had been a fantasy world for me. I had heard no world news so had no knowledge of the war, death, misery and destruction that had continued during the four months I had been away. In my world there had principally been utter peace, beauty and endless amounts of grace. Ignorance can definitely be bliss. But only for a time. I knew I would soon need a reality check.

The aftermath of 11 September included events that had no meaning in my waterworld. We had flown to Tenerife shortly after that dreadful day, and thus missed much of the immediate news coverage. A journalist from *The Times* had asked me mid-Atlantic how I felt about it. My response shocked me. I had not thought about it at all and explained that I could not recognise any real personal emotional response to the disaster. I remained shocked by my answer for days afterwards. Why could I feel nothing? It was so unlike me. Certainly, being so far removed from anyone or anything made it hard to relate to events on dry land, however terrible. I could conclude only that it was my lack of exposure to the media that had left me devoid of any real response.

One day towards the end of November, the *Times* journalist called again. That morning, he explained, had been the first since 11 September that *The Times* had not run the terrorist attacks as the front-page story. The other broadsheets had given it the same coverage and I knew it must have dominated the TV news. I realised then that being unable to read the facts was less important. It was the TV images and raw human emotion before my eyes that I had missed. I was unable to empathise because my emotions had been unable to connect, via those pictures, with the suffering. No one could fail to be moved by the images of the Twin Towers and the helplessness and horror that had been felt by the people of New York, and the world beyond.

Images are often more powerful than words and have the ability to rouse our emotions in a way words might not. Before I left England I had cried for the people of New York as I watched those images. I also cried for an Afghan woman and her family, victims of war, eating grass to survive. Yet at sea, without the images to stir my emotions so deeply, I found it was possible to forget. Proof perhaps of the power, and responsibility, carried by the media.

I had thought about the media more and more as my voyage progressed. The closer I got to Barbados, the more interested the media became in my own story. By Wednesday, the day Andrew arrived, representatives from four national British newspapers, a host of local journalists and a team from the BBC had arrived in Port St Charles. Andrew felt very odd as a BBC cameraman filmed him as he walked off the aeroplane. The rest of the passengers looked on, wondering which megastar they were failing to recognise!

Teresa and Rachel from the Challenge Business had already called one press conference in Barbados when I was still three days from land. They relayed stories of the atmosphere in Port St Charles on the phone to me, describing it as 'electric'. Two Barbadian newspapers published articles on my finish, asking everyone to head for North Beach to wave me in on Saturday morning. The same message was given out on *Good Morning, Barbados*, the most popular morning TV show on the island. There was even a rumour that the prime minister of Barbados was coming to present me with my finishing award at a cocktail party held in my honour on the following Monday evening!

Apart from wondering how I'd iron a cocktail dress on board *Troika* in readiness, I was astounded that my little row had created such interest. I felt extremely honoured but slightly bemused and embarrassed. Again, I wondered if maybe the enormity of what I was achieving had yet to register with me. I was still far too busy with the day-to-day business of getting there!

Receiving media attention was something I felt extremely nervous about. I was worried about how I would cope with up-close cameras and crowds after having spent so much time alone. Yet I was indebted to our sponsors, Troika, and wanted to get them as much publicity as I could.

I had no idea what to expect, or where it would all lead, but if there were fresh opportunities I knew I must make the most of them. I was sure the attention wouldn't last long. Stories like mine, I thought, are always short-lived. Perhaps Andy Warhol was right – everyone has his or her fifteen minutes of fame and this was to be mine. I set about getting *Troika* ready for her big finale.

I scrubbed her decks and completed all the little jobs that I had been meaning to do for months. I knew it was pointless polishing her, with consistent force six to seven conditions and force-eight squalls passing through regularly, covering her with salt. But I was so boat-proud I couldn't resist! I, too, needed a bit of sorting out. I washed some clothes to put on, chuckling to myself that, if I really wanted to get *Troika* big publicity, perhaps I should row into Port St Charles naked as usual!

Hayley, being the most thoughtful person in the word, had included a razor and sachets of hair moisturiser and conditioner for sun-bleached hair in my Christmas parcel. It was time to make myself look presentable. Shaving my legs after four months was comical. Each inch took at least fifteen strokes, with the razor clogging up after the second stroke. It was blunt after half a leg! It had been great not having to bow to the pressure of what a Western woman should look like for a few months. Not worrying what you look like is liberating, but now I enjoyed pampering myself again. I even brushed my hair, which I hadn't done for weeks.

With 24 hours to go, both *Troika* and I were looking far more presentable, but things were not looking so good on the navigation front. Concerned that I was going to be blown too far south, I held off as much as I could, and managed to keep eight to ten nautical miles between me and the position at which I hoped to round North Point. My plan was to go with the wind throughout the last sixteen hours and head down to one nautical mile offshore. If it worked, there would be enough clearance between *Troika* and the rocks at North Point. I would be in a suitable position to slip around the top to the lee side, away from the rolling Atlantic, towards the shelter of the land. It would then be only a few hours' rowing down the lee sides to Port St Charles.

But with 24 hours to go, the wind changed direction and pushed me directly west, and occasionally north of west. My plan was backfiring. I was heading for St Lucia after all.

✉

D, Left hand down a bit, more
effort bow side pls. St Lucia dead
ahead! I know I said it was nice
but . . . Love Barney

Phone calls to the race HQ, and also to Andrew, confirmed my worst fears.

'Hi, Teresa, it's Debra.'

Teresa knows me well and I knew she would immediately pick up on my less than buoyant tone of voice. Sure enough, she asked if everything was OK.

'Not really. I've just been looking at the chart and doing the calculations. I think I may need a tow.'

'I think you will,' Teresa replied. 'I've just had a meeting with Lin [skipper of *Challenge Yacht 47*] and she'd come to the same conclusion.'

We discussed that I would need towing from whichever point I crossed the finish line down to Port St Charles. Otherwise I would quickly be washed past the island. There was no way in the conditions – still force six to seven – that I would be able to row across the waves and down the lee side.

The idea of being towed in, in front of my family, press photographers and local supporters was humiliating. I just hoped everyone would understand why. What a way to be welcomed after all I had been through! There was nothing I could do but get on with it. The rest of my family were flying out that day. Knowing I would be with them soon in the arrival scene I had mentally rehearsed so many times soon eased any heartache I had over a tow.

The rest of the day was spent trying to get a visual on the island. Other crews had told me that they had been able to see Barbados with around 25 miles to go. As I was ready to reach dry land I was looking forward to that first satisfying glimpse. But, as the day stretched on, I still couldn't see the island. I wasn't worried, as I felt confident in my navigation and knew it was out there somewhere. I needed that glimpse for satisfaction more than anything else, so every few strokes I would look over my shoulder, scanning the horizon. But all I could see was a bank of cloud. Cloud shapes kept teasing, convincing me that they were Barbados, as I didn't really know what it would look like. I wasn't sure whether I was looking for a pimple on the horizon or a long, flat slice of land.

$\boxtimes$

```
Debra, as a reminder, land is a
different colour. Doesn't move, has
people on it and smells different!
Tim [Troika]
```

At sunset my waiting was over. As the sun shone through the bank of cloud a silhouette of the island seemed to appear from nowhere and suddenly looked as if it were right next to me – a surprisingly long, flat, slice.

As darkness fell, I was left gazing at Barbados, like a glittering prize set in front of me. I really was going to make it.

Yet instead of being elated I began to feel uncomfortable. Frightened, even. I realised I was scared of returning to dry land, of being part of a crowd, of the sights and sounds to which I'd grown unaccustomed, the demands and routine of 'society'.

I had become so used to my solitary world on the beautiful ocean in *Troika*: the constant motion and natural sounds; being hit by flying fish and chased by turtles; my routine of two hours on, one hour off; not wearing any clothes and not having to care, and most importantly not having anyone around whose expectations I felt I had to live up to.

I had grown completely accustomed to life on board. It was what I knew best. I understood how to respond to the boat and the conditions, but life on land had become alien to me. I had loved living in a world filled with grace and was concerned about returning to a dog-eat-dog society.

I became upset about having to face the waiting media. What if the press became intrusive? What if I couldn't cope with being surrounded by people again? What if I suffered with land sickness? I was bound to have problems walking, and normal food and drink was going to take some getting used to.

I sat in the darkness, watching the lights of Barbados grow increasingly brighter, and felt strangely melancholy. My friends and family had landed a few hours earlier and I knew they were at Cath and Thomas's house, waiting for me to call. What kind of welcome was I giving them if I shared my fears? I was so excited about seeing them all, but it wasn't just them I would be seeing. I didn't want the press to intrude on our family reunion. I felt very emotional.

I called the house and spoke to Mum. Keeping the strange mix of emotion from my voice was very difficult. She sounded so happy and I could hear all the excited noises from the others in the background.

'How was your flight, Mum?' I wanted to ask her direct questions so she wouldn't ask me too many. I knew I couldn't hold it together if she asked me how I was.

She said it had been fine and gave me a few details.

'We can't wait to see you tomorrow, darling. It's going to be so exciting.'

I squirmed a 'Me too, Mum' reply and abruptly stopped as a big lump formed in my throat.

When Mum passed the phone to Hayley, I burst into tears. Would Hayley make sense of this for me? As I sobbed down the phone, she gently assured me that my mixed emotions were to be expected. 'It wouldn't be normal if you didn't feel this way,' she said. 'It's your big day ahead and we'll do whatever you want to do. You certainly won't have to do anything you're not comfortable with.'

I knew that the one thing I wanted to do was be with my family.

Andrew was next on the line with more reassurance. He explained that the pontoon I was landing on was not open to the press or public, so I wasn't going to be surrounded by people.

'It'll only be me, Sir Chay and some VIPs on the pontoon, Debs, and once you get through customs there'll be an area cordoned off for us all to get together.'

I was relieved that I'd at least be able to meet my family in private.

'Teresa and Rachel have done a great job organising things. There's a structured timetable for meetings with the press, so we can all go off to the Pool Bar together for half an hour before the press conference. Don't worry, everything's under control.'

I was relieved but still very emotional. Only thirty minutes with my family before I had to face the press. I had slept only a few hours in the nights leading up to the finish and lack of sleep was making me feel fragile again.

I curled up in a ball and held Woody the bear tightly, feeling intensely vulnerable.

The tiredness became worse, as I didn't want to fall asleep on the last night and drift onto the rocks. I was too excited and nervous to sleep, anyway. I was due to cross the finish line at approximately 5 a.m. Andrew and I had discussed the option of having the family all come out on boats to be at the line of longitude that would be my finish, but the conditions were appalling. It would not have been safe, and I would be crossing the finishing line in the dark – not great for spectators.

✉

Debs, big hug waiting, although if you could arrive later in the afternoon so we could have a lie-in that would be great! L.o.l, Matt

Things were about to go crazy on the media front. Little did I know that *The Times* had hit the newsstands with a large picture of me on the front page. It was still 2 a.m. local time for me, but 6 a.m. in England. Breakfast-time television shows had just started and a review of the papers exposed my story. A text message soon arrived from BBC Breakfast News asking if I was prepared to do a live phone interview. As I was up anyway, I thought I might as well. I quite liked the idea of having a practice interview before reaching the journalists on land. What I didn't realise was that all TV and radio news programmes watch and listen to each other. As soon as I had finished the BBC interview, I was bombarded with phone calls and text messages asking for more. I gave interviews throughout the early hours of the morning, but it was not until one presenter said, 'Do you realise what big news you are back home? You are the toast of Great Britain today!' that I realised just how huge the story had become. I was stunned.

✉

That sound in the background is a host of fat ladies in rehearsal. Remember it ain't over 'till they sing! Adrian xxx

My anxieties about facing the media had become much less intense after the phone interviews. To my surprise I had found it easy, almost enjoyable. After all, they were only asking me questions about my Atlantic crossing, and it was a topic that I knew inside and out, but my journey was far from over and the fat ladies definitely weren't singing. I still had my finish line to cross. I approached 57 degrees 37 minutes west, sitting alone in the dark, feeling calm. I didn't even notice the wind and the waves as I soaked in the peace and tranquillity of the ocean for one last time. As I drifted across the finish line I didn't cheer, punch the air, or yell with triumph. I just smiled a broad smile of contentment. This was how it was meant to be, I thought – just me, Woody and beautiful *Troika*. Crossing the line that way seemed perfect. I was filled with that special, quiet contentment that had been such an important discovery for me during the months alone at sea. It was a fitting end. With Dad as my inspiration, I felt I could not have failed. He would have been so proud of my achievement.

Having enjoyed my own solitary moments, I immediately wanted to share them with Andrew. It was quarter to five in the morning but I knew this was one phone call he wouldn't mind being woken up by. As he answered sleepily, I began to sing: '59 degrees 37 minutes,

59 degrees 37 minutes, ee-ay-ipio, 59 degrees 37 minutes!' I could almost hear the smile on his face, and the delight in his voice filled me with joy. I felt overwhelmed with love for him. We had made it.

By dawn I could see the mast light of the Challenge yacht sailing towards me. My patience was fast running out. I was desperate to see Andrew, but being towed across the waves in those conditions was not going to be easy. I needed all my strength and alertness for seeing *Troika* in, and I knew I shouldn't waste it on impatience. The Challenge Business crew sensibly waited for daylight before attempting to set up the tow, but I was eager to get going.

Trying to throw a rope from a large yacht to a small rowing boat in a big swell is by no means easy and it took a number of attempts. With everything necessary attached, I crouched in the foot well with a steering line in each hand and prepared myself for a bumpy ride.

As the yacht towed me along, the waves crashed over *Troika* and I was soaked within minutes. I needn't have bothered washing and brushing my hair after all! We made good speed until I surfed too quickly across a wave towards the yacht. The towing rope sank as the distance between the two crafts reduced. But as they pulled away, the rope looped around *Troika*'s keel and started to pull her over. As capsize looked imminent, I realised I was in for a more dramatic finish than I had expected, but the fatal moment was saved by quick thinking from the crew. I could hear Gavin shouting, 'Release the line! Release the line!' With the towing line freed, *Troika* fell back on to a level keel with a crash.

Shortly after a new line was set up and towing had resumed, the first boat full of well-wishers arrived. I felt myself begin to panic and had to repeat quietly to myself, 'Keep calm, Debra, they are here to welcome you.' As I choked back the tears, I wanted to scream to the yacht to turn around and tow me back out. I knew I was being ridiculous and battled to compose myself.

I also felt embarrassed. Embarrassed to be seen being towed and hoping desperately that we would reach the drop-off point before my family arrived in Thomas's boat. No such luck. As we reached the

lee side of the island, the conditions were still bad. I was disappointed that the sea wasn't more sheltered by the land. There was
no way I was going to be able to row in the offshore conditions. The
wind was funnelling over the top of the island and I would be blown
towards the Caribbean Sea very quickly unless they towed me right
in and dropped me outside the marina entrance. There was no
avoiding it. I had to get used to the embarrassment. Everyone was
going to see me being towed.

The next boat to hurtle towards me carried a familiar crowd in
matching blue tops – my friends and family in their *Troika* supporters' kit. They all hung over the side, waving like mad and
completely soaked. High-speed and big waves had caused a lot of
spray, but they didn't seem to care. They were all so happy and
as I looked at each of their faces I felt that we had never spent a
moment apart.

The expression on Andrew's face was wonderful, full of pride, joy
and relief. He mouthed 'I love you' and I just wanted to leap off the
boat, swim over to him and tell him that I loved him too. But my
hands were full of steering lines. Just waving back was impossible, as
I couldn't drop the lines. All I could do was sit there and grin from
under the hood of my waterproofs. That was not how I had imagined
the moment would be!

More and more boats surrounded us as we sped along towards
Port St Charles, accompanied by shouting and horn blowing. No one
seemed to care that I was being towed. Perhaps they understood
why. Their buoyant mood was contagious. I soon forgot my
embarrassment and started enjoying my surroundings, determined
to take in every detail.

Two kayakers joined me. They must have come miles and were
really paddling hard to keep up with us. I couldn't believe that so
many people had come to see me in, despite the rain and choppy
conditions. The atmosphere was amazing. Far from feeling nervous
with so many people, as I'd expected, their smiling faces and warm
welcome started to make me feel at ease.

As we approached the entrance to Port St Charles, I could see hundreds of people lining the helipad on the quayside. Hayley was right. This was going to be my day – a day to remember.

The Challenge yacht dropped the tow just outside the entrance to Port St Charles and I came to a stop. Boats were coming right up with congratulations, as I scrambled out of my Musto smock and prepared for the last row of my epic voyage.

I looked across to my family. They were holding up a huge sheet on the bow of the boat, which read COME IN NO. 22. YOUR TIME IS UP.

How right they were. It was time to come in and bring my amazing adventure to a close.

✉

Debra, You've been in that boat nearly half my life! Love Tilly Mason aged 7^1/$_2$ months

Chapter 9

Barbados –
Entry by Sea

I was still fifty metres from land, but microphones were already being thrust in my face. Photographers were hanging from small speedboats, shouting, 'Debra! Debra! This way! This way!' and 'Look like you're *really* pulling hard!'

I *was* pulling hard – I just don't pull a contorted face when I do! I had no option other than to pull hard at this point, as I was going nowhere fast. Each stroke felt as if I were rowing into a brick wall, and I was getting redder in the face with the exertion. Everyone was cheering and blowing horns, but my excitement was beginning to drain away. Instead, my frustration was mounting as the wind tried to prevent me from covering those final metres. In addition, posing for photos had slowed me down and was distracting me from the task.

My two kayaking buddies stayed next to me, guiding me in. I was so grateful for their company and guidance. I kept asking, 'Do you think I'm actually making any progress?' They assured me that I was and gave me even more encouragement.

The BBC crew came alongside with Andrew, who had somehow switched to their boat. He was so close now that I just wanted to get to the quayside so that I could give him a hug, but the headwind meant that *Troika* was hardly moving.

Robert Hall, the BBC reporter, pointed a microphone in my direction and asked, 'How're you feeling, Debra? What's it like to see Andrew again?'

These were major questions and I desperately wanted to say something dramatic and poignant. But at that moment I couldn't concentrate on questions – all I felt was concern that I wasn't going to make it to the quay. I was out of breath, bright red in the face and about to make a complete idiot of myself by not being able to row the last few metres to land – not exactly great viewing for the folks back home! I struggled to say something coherent between gasps for air, but my mumbling can't have been the striking sound bite he was hoping to hear.

Those last metres took forever and I wondered whether the crowds on the helipad were tapping their feet and twiddling their thumbs as they waited. The press boats all shot off to get to the quay to take some photographs, and I was left with my kayaking friends and the Challenge yacht.

The Challenge skipper, Lin, came alongside.

'Debra?' she yelled. 'Do you want another tow?'

'Not just yet, Lin,' I managed between strokes. 'Give me a few more minutes.'

'OK.' She grinned. 'We'll be right here. If you keep your hull parallel with us, you'll follow the line you need to take.'

'Thanks,' I shouted back to her. The skipper and crew of the Challenge yacht had been brilliant throughout the race. I could see from their faces that they really wanted me to make it. They understood my determination.

I started driving with my legs as hard as I could. It was easier without the interruptions from the press. As I rowed, they were frantically setting up on the quay, ready for my arrival. I started to creep forwards, willing myself with each stroke. As I approached the helipad, I was more sheltered from the wind and rowing began to get a bit easier. The boat picked up speed and at last I was getting there. The atmosphere was electric. The crowd cheered. I could feel every one of them willing me on.

As I reached the helipad, I jumped off my seat and grabbed a spare oar that was lying on the deck next to me. This was my opportunity to give a victory salute and I felt I had earned the right to take it. I lifted the oar above my head and a deafening cheer erupted. The crowd went wild and boats everywhere blew their horns raucously. The noise was unbelievable. The feeling of satisfaction amazing. My happiness complete. I had done it.

I had rowed the Atlantic Ocean – for Dad, for my family, for Matt Jess, for Andrew and for me.

I had dared to dream. And my dream had come true.

My senses suddenly kicked in, released by the relief of arrival. Each one competed with another, sharpening my experience. The scent of the crowd and the land was heady. The vibrant colours – after shades of blue and grey for months – were almost startling. But the incredible noise won easily. I still had to row around the pontoon, under the bow of a 120-foot super-yacht. It sounded its horn and I could feel the noise vibrating in my lungs. Every one of my senses was so acute. It was like being reborn and experiencing each one for the first time. I felt so alive.

As I rounded the super-yachts, I could see Andrew and Sir Chay Blyth waiting for me. I was so eager to get to Andrew that I wasn't really concentrating on steering the boat and almost rammed the pontoon! But there were others ready to pull *Troika Transatlantic* in.

As I came alongside, Chay let loose with a bottle of champagne – with me as a target – and hit the bull's-eye. As I wiped the champagne from my eyes, Andrew was right there in front of me. He reached down into the boat and put his arms around me to give me a huge hug. I didn't notice the people, the cameras or the BBC microphone pinned to Andrew's shirt. I was only aware of his arms around me, and the warm and wonderful sense – keener than all the others – that I was now safe.

'You made it!' were Andrew's first words to me. 'No – we made it,' I said, and hugged him hard.

I had known the ultimate adventure. I had seen awesome wildlife, survived more than enough scary moments and had done an enormous amount of soul searching – but nothing could beat the feeling of being back in Andrew's arms.

After a minute of hugging, a persistent noise started to break through. Photographers were yelling at the VIPs on the pontoon. The press were all located across a small stretch of water on some rocks and the small crowd on the pontoon were blocking their shot. The tone of their voices startled me as they repeatedly shouted, 'Get out of the way!' Everyone was after that special shot and they were getting increasingly frustrated. Hearing so many voices was weird after so long and perhaps I had forgotten how powerfully – and angrily – they could be used. So this was life in front of a press pack!

Attempting to walk on dry land was hilarious. My calf muscles had wasted away, and my ability to balance had gone with them. It really was the strangest sensation. I just couldn't stand up if I wasn't holding onto someone or something. Even then, I would be fine one minute and on the floor the next after my knees had buckled and my calves could not rectify the situation. For over three months my body had constantly had to adjust its position in relation to the movement of the boat on the waves. Now that I was back on dry land, my body was anticipating surface movement that was lacking. It would take a further two weeks before I would stop moving unnecessarily.

I had to go through customs before I was allowed to see the rest of my family. I wobbled and swayed my way into the customs building on the shoulder of Teresa, the race manager, as Andrew was not allowed in with me. The office was air-conditioned, the mood serious and quiet. I sat down to sign some papers but was on such a high that all I wanted to do was talk. And talk I did – incessantly. I was so excited that I couldn't concentrate. Needless to say, the customs officers weren't very amused! They repeatedly put papers in front of me with the instruction, 'Sign and date please.' Each time I couldn't remember how to sign my name and kept forgetting the date. I shivered from the air conditioning, having not experienced cold air for four months, but nothing could chill the warm grin on my face. The stamp the customs officer thumped on to my passport seemed to seal my arrival, top my excitement, and master the art of understatement. It read: BARBADOS – ENTRY BY SEA.

When I emerged from the customs office, I was met by that familiar crowd of *Troika*-blue shirts, very pale skin and big smiles. This was the moment I had dreamed of so often when life at sea got tough. With the fulfilment of that dream, the tough times seemed to melt away. I didn't know whom to hug first, so started with the nearest – Mum.

We have always been a close family but had grown even closer throughout the voyage. This was one of the many unexpected joys it brought. The family had been communicating more frequently, in general, as each member rang Hayley and Andrew to receive updates on my progress. Hugging Mum felt fantastic. I felt as if I had really got to know her, and that she had come to understand me while I had been away. We had developed a deeper understanding of each other and this meant the world to me.

My friend Joanna was crying again. She had been crying when I had last seen her in Tenerife and I hoped she hadn't been crying the whole time I had been away! Pete was the giant cuddly bear he always was and I was overjoyed that they had flown all the way to the Caribbean to see me in. They had been about to move house and could ill afford the fare, and the fact that Pete had had to face his fear of flying made their big commitment to my finish all the more special. Leigh had been given a rare few days off from Mount House School in Devon to fly out for the finish. It meant so much to me that the headmaster was sympathetic to our family situation in allowing him the time. It wouldn't have been the same without him.

The press and Barbadian supporters were on the other side of the customs building, so it was suggested that I could sneak out the other way. It was tempting, but somehow seemed heartless. The Barbadians and residents of Port St Charles had given me a welcome beyond my wildest dreams. I couldn't ignore it. Facing the crowds didn't seem so hard with Andrew by my side. As we rounded the building and ducked under the barrier, the press encircled us. Andrew pulled me in close to him and I automatically felt protected.

I had forgotten just how comforting it was to be held by someone who is six foot five! He towered above most of the reporters, making me feel very secure.

Meeting the little children who had come to greet me was brilliant, even if it was a little odd when they asked for my autograph! I couldn't get my head around suddenly being famous. Kate, a young girl who had emailed me, had travelled up with her parents from the south of the island. I was really looking forward to meeting her to thank her for her support. Kate gave me a beautiful bowl, made on the island, and a copy of a speech she had read to her class about how much she respected me for carrying on when Andrew was unable to. I felt completely humbled by that ten-year-old.

We eventually retreated to Chay's apartment, where a hot bath was waiting for me, along with a journalist from a national newspaper. They were going to cover the story exclusively and wanted an early interview. Reacquainting myself with my family was going to have to wait. At least Andrew was still next to me, and I was on such a high that I really didn't mind who else was there.

But first things first: I couldn't wait to luxuriate in a hot bath after nearly four months without washing facilities. Hayley had organised toiletries and clean clothes – what a star! I stripped off my rowing kit and was astounded by my reflection in the full-length mirror. My body had changed shape and I hardly recognised the person staring back at me. My legs had wasted away and I looked so toned. I hadn't realised how tanned I was until I stood next to Hayley, whose skin had not seen the sun for months. No wonder everyone kept telling me that I looked as if I had just got back from three months on a health farm!

The bath was blissful but followed by panic, as the scum from my unwashed body stuck like cement to the side of the bath. There were no cleaning materials and Chay had specifically stressed that, as it was not his apartment, we were to leave it in the condition we found it in. Much frenzied scrubbing with toilet paper ensued!

Smelling significantly better and having completed the interview, I headed out for the next round of TV and radio interviews, followed by a small press conference. I hadn't been expecting such intense media attention.

By the time we got back to my family at the Pool Bar, everyone was looking relaxed, but tired. The bar was excellent for inducing a state of relaxation, mostly due to the endless flow of drinks served by the charismatic barman, Ian. Everyone was tucking into fabulous barbecued food, which I knew would be a problem for me. I would have to break into rich foods gently. I wanted to start with something easy like a banana, but got more than I bargained for when a large banana-daiquiri cocktail was put in front of me. I thought, this is my kind of place! It seemed almost surreal. Only hours before, I had been alone on a small boat out at sea while my family were on the exotic island of Barbados. Now I was on 'the other side' of the contrast with them, watching them all, smiling and chatting.

Troika had been moved to the pontoon by the bar and I felt a pang of sadness to see her there. Having spent so long sitting in her looking outwards I felt uncomfortable to be sitting outside looking in. She had protected me through an endless barrage of force-eight squalls, particularly in the final three weeks. For a small plywood boat she was pretty tough. I had an urge to take my banana daiquiri and sit in her once more – but it was time for both of us to move on. She would be heading back in a container ship to a good home soon, that of her original owners: Miles Barnett, the RAF pilot who had been unable to get leave, and his rowing partner, Alan Watson. Having missed out on the 2001–2 race, they hoped to row her in the next Challenge Business Atlantic Rowing Race to raise money for cancer research. Knowing this before I left Tenerife had been a great motivator. Giving up would have meant burning the boat at sea and I couldn't let that happen. With Andrew and I both having lost our fathers to cancer, we were delighted with her future role

As I enjoyed the company of my family, I thought of all the other people who had supported me throughout my journey, and helped to keep the oars in motion: those who had written text messages and Christmas cards, those who had sent presents, those who had posted words of encouragement on the website. They were with me right to the end. I found their final messages moving beyond words and they reminded me, yet again, that my journey was not just about a girl in a small rowing boat:

> ✉
>
> Can't think of a word to sum up what you have achieved. Well done seems too small. What I would like to say is thank you. U have been a real inspiration 2 me. Always gave me a real boost 2 come back from dialysis and read your latest diary. After missing out on the BT Global Challenge I love to see people getting out there and living their dreams. What a story you have told! Thanks for being so honest with us. Easy to hide behind emails, so v. brave not 2 do so. Enjoy the buzz, you deserve it so much. Thanks again for being such an inspiration. Speak soon (somehow!) Matt Jess.

> ✉
>
> Those of us whose daily grind is lifted by tracking your progress will miss you! Gill Lumsdon

I imagined Dad, sitting with us, the life and soul of the party, as always. But for the first time I didn't painfully wish him there. I had learned to draw inspiration from the past – and from Dad – to live for today and look forward to the future. I felt terrific. But my mood was about to be tested. I was about to get my first close-up of life in the lens of the media – and it was not a pretty sight.

Mark Pepper, a friend and independent British photographer who had journeyed out to shoot my finish, joined us at the Pool Bar. I was delighted he had made it, as he had supported me with text messages throughout my adventure. Mark wanted to take some photographs of Andrew and me together and of me with my family. I was happy to oblige. However, the photographer from the national paper we'd arranged the exclusive deal with was getting twitchy. He interrupted with, 'I'm sorry. I can't let you take those photos.'

Mark explained that he would use the pictures only for magazines due out after the national paper had run their story, but the other photographer was not convinced. He didn't know Mark. If he had, he wouldn't have worried, as Mark is a man true to his word. The photographer from the national paper was only doing his job and protecting his exclusivity, but nevertheless the atmosphere became very awkward. I stepped away and sat on the edge of the pool. I was determined not to get involved. My minor celebrity status didn't strike me as something that would lead to altercations between members of the media, but this was my first brush with fame and I didn't realise what a coup it was for a newspaper to obtain an exclusive. Andrew and the photographer had a brief discussion and Andrew returned with a compromise: Mark was allowed to take photos of me on my own.

After a little relaxation we were needed for another interview for the exclusive. Andrew and I had not yet had the opportunity to talk everything through face to face, so we were anxious about sharing all our thoughts with a journalist. After the heightened emotions of the day and my physical exhaustion, reliving our experiences and going though everything in minute detail was emotionally draining. The journalist's apartment overlooked the Pool Bar, where our family were waiting for us, and we became increasingly restless. But a BBC TV interview was set up for us next.

I really wasn't prepared for the extent of the media interest in us. My family had flown so far to be with me, but now I was beginning to wonder whether I was going to have a holiday with them or with journalists and photographers! Time with my family was to be minimal for the first few days on dry land – that was the cost of all the publicity we received. We didn't realise at the time that it would be of great benefit to us.

The journalists from the national paper with the 'exclusive' deal accompanied us wherever we went – they had to make the most of their story – but I found it hard to believe that there were other journalists who were sneaking around with cameras, trying to get photos of Andrew and me together. Restaurants, bars, BBC interviews – wherever we went they went too. It got to the point where we started to invite them along! At least that way it was out in the open and we didn't feel as though we were being secretly watched.

The media world is a staggering one to walk into unprepared. Unlike those who enter *Big Brother*-type TV programmes in an attempt to find their fifteen minutes of fame, we had not entered the race for big publicity. We'd naturally hoped for coverage for *Troika* and her namesake sponsors – that's how sponsorship works. But we could never have anticipated the attention we received – and continue to receive – from the media. It was almost like going to a new school: at first we didn't know the rules or the norms or how to respond to the new environment and people. We had been plunged in at the deep end, but we were learning to swim fast.

On Sunday morning we heard that our story was featured in almost every national Sunday paper in the UK, and was front-page news in many. We later heard that the story made the front page of several newspapers for three days in a row. We were astounded by all this.

The broadsheets had presented a healthy reflection on Andrew's exit from the race, balancing it with a clear focus on my achievement. Unfortunately, many of the tabloids had chosen to focus on Andrew's 'abandoning' me. I felt like phoning them to shout, 'It wasn't like that! He did not abandon me! I *chose* to go on alone!' But I remembered some sound advice Chay Blyth had given us soon after the finish. In his gruff Scottish accent, he said, 'Never believe your own publicity and don't read any negative articles written about you.'

The way in which Andrew handled the publicity impressed me. If the situation had been reversed, I certainly would not have coped as well and would have found it hard not to take it personally. He explained his reaction wonderfully in an update for the website.

Website update from Andrew Veal - 15 December 2001

. . . I hadn't expected to kick off quite such a palaver by telling a couple of journalists that the reason I got off was because I was scared! There hasn't been a single friend, relative, person whose views I would normally care about, or anyone from the race itself, who has been anything other than extremely supportive and understanding about the whole thing. Most have taken the 'At least you tried' approach, while one or two have gone so far as to say, 'It's a lot braver just to say you had a real problem with it than to pretend you were injured or something.'

However, I guess that doesn't make for good headlines, so there will no doubt continue to be some mildly embarrassing press coverage. But if it brings Debra recognition, it doesn't really matter if a few people whose idea of a big adventure is a rollercoaster ride want to make a big thing out of it. It's at times like these that you really appreciate your friends and, I have to say, I've got some great ones.

Thanks to you all.

Andrew.

The irony was that the main reason why the story became so big was because a husband dropped out and his wife had continued. Had it been the other way around, I don't suppose we would even have made our local newspaper back home. This speaks volumes about what society expects, or does not expect, from a woman. Andrew had done the unexpected by openly admitting he had a fear, and I had done the same by continuing beyond a point where a man could not. There is a part of me, albeit a small part, that feels bitter about all the attention being mainly due to the fact that I am a woman, and less to do with the fact that I have rowed an ocean.

I wouldn't say that I'm a raging feminist. I hold relatively traditional views on male and female roles. But the perspective that many people took of my adventure has really opened my eyes to the way that women, and female adventurers in particular, are viewed and portrayed in society. Kate Shaw, our literary agent, sent me a saying by the famous mountaineer Tenzing Norgay to the effect that it is the hearts of men that make Everest big or small. She then made an observation that all the best quotations always seemed to be about men. This really got me thinking. I went back through all the inspiring quotations people had texted to me while I was at sea and only one out of the 77 I was sent mentions women, rather than men.

$$\boxtimes$$

'I have met brave women who are exploring the outer edge of human possibility, with no history to guide them and with a courage to make themselves vulnerable that I found moving beyond words.'
Gloria Steinem

The media often overlook female adventurers for a whole host of reasons, but, when one of us does get recognition, the exposure is often vast. Ellen MacArthur, the talented yachtswoman, is a good example of how the media have positively highlighted the achievements of a young woman who chased her dreams and achieved a great feat. She is a truly fantastic role model for young people, so the exposure benefits many. But I wonder whether the exposure is in recognition of the achievement or of the fact that the achiever is a woman. I'd like to hope a yacht*sman* in the same position would attract equal attention.

There was no doubt about it – the wife-braver-than-husband storyline was a great publicity spinner and if I wanted to benefit from media exposure, I had to play on the fact that I am a woman. There was an element of having to toe the line in order to be able to put the real story across.

Television shows soon tracked us down in Barbados to offer all kinds of incentives to fly back to the UK for an interview. Initially we had agreed not to fly back for interviews until we had enjoyed a holiday together and with our family, the risk being that the story would be old news by then and we would have missed out on a number of unique opportunities. Then something happened to change our minds.

Two days after I had finished the race, Andrew went to take a call by the Pool Bar. He came back grinning in disbelief. 'It's the Johnny Vaughan show. They want to know if we'll fly back tomorrow to appear on *Johnny Vaughan Tonight* with Meg Ryan.' I could see Andrew was trying very hard to keep the grin off his face as he spoke! It was so unreal that we could do nothing but laugh at the ridiculousness of it all. We weren't celebrities. We were just a couple who had a dream to row across the Atlantic. We weren't exactly in Meg Ryan's league!

'But our families are here,' I reminded Andrew. 'They've come all this way to be with us. How can we fly back to England and leave them here?'

'I told the researchers that – and they said they'd fly all of us back to England, put them up in a hotel after they've watched the show and then fly us all back the next day!'

I immediately wondered whether they knew just how many

family members we had with us on Barbados! 'That's crazy. They don't need to do that.'

'Well, what do you want to do?' Andrew asked.

'The viewing figures for a show with Meg Ryan as the guest will be huge,' Hayley suggested. 'It would be a good one to do.'

So, 36 hours later, Andrew and I were sitting together in the first-class section of a Virgin Atlantic flight bound for Heathrow. As the rest of the passengers slept, I sat in my extra-wide chair eating a fine selection of my favourite cheeses and drinking a glass of red wine. I had solid-silver salt and pepper pots and heavy silver cutlery on the tray in front of me. Where was my favourite orange plastic spoon now?

I used to dream of cheese and a glass of red wine as I forced down the beef stew and dumplings. The stewardesses had even put a tablecloth on my foldaway tray! It all just seemed too much. As if one adventure was over, and a whole new one was starting. The enormity of it all had finally hit me. I was back in the real world – a world of people, material possessions and complexities. I wondered how long it would be before I would start taking life, and the simple things in it, for granted once again.

As I nibbled my cheese and sipped wine I watched the monitor in front of me, not showing the in-flight movie, but a map. The Caribbean was shown on the left and Europe on the right with the blue Atlantic Ocean in between. A line of dots followed by a small flashing plane signified where we had got to in our journey. It even told me how many miles we had travelled across the Atlantic – 1,600. It had taken us a matter of hours to cover the same distance it had taken me two months to row. The walls of irony were closing in on all sides. The contrast was phenomenal.

✉

D, I just read that Concorde flies once a week to Barbados. Amazing to go one way in 112 days and back in 5 hours! Love Barney

I felt overwhelmed with the need to talk to someone. I had dozens of people around me, but they were all asleep, as was Andrew. I could see the stewardesses in their work area through the gap in the curtain. With their passengers asleep they were chatting together about their day. I wanted to talk to them but could imagine how crazy it would sound: 'I hope you don't mind but I've just got to talk to someone. I've been alone at sea for three months and am desperate for some company. Would you mind if I joined you?' I watched them for half an hour, struggling to work up the courage to wander along and join in the gossip. Eventually a stewardess got edgy about me staring at them and yanked the curtain closed. No, she definitely wouldn't have understood.

Everyone at the BBC and at World's End (the production company) was exceptionally friendly and welcoming. They seemed genuinely interested in the story – amazing when they also had a star like Meg Ryan on the show. Like all megastars, she wafted in with an entourage of people, already late for an interview in Paris. She looked exhausted from the flight but still radiated beauty and seemed as sweet as all of the characters she has played in her romantic comedies. She seemed riveted by what we had to say, staggered that I had spent so much time on my own.

Walking through Heathrow airport the following day was very odd. Everywhere we went we could hear people whispering, 'That's the couple that were on the Johnny Vaughan show last night'. One couple stopped to ask us all about it as we waited to put our hand luggage through the scanner. I felt quite relieved to be heading back to Barbados, as being recognised was something I hadn't considered.

At the airport back in Barbados, where the press were waiting, there was a rumour circulating that Meg Ryan's production company were interested in buying the rights to our story. By the time this had been passed by Chinese whispers, the tabloids were reporting that Meg Ryan was going to play me in the film version of the story and that the filming schedule was already under way! I can no longer read a newspaper without feeling extremely sceptical.

Finally, we were back in Barbados with our families and friends
and the journalists went home. Andrew and I still hadn't really had
the opportunity to spend any quality time alone and we were keen
to talk through everything that had happened. We also needed to
reconsider our plans for the future, as lots of doors were beginning
to open as a result of all the publicity. We had hoped that the flights
to London and back would give us such an opportunity, but Andrew
had been so exhausted that he couldn't even finish his in-flight meal
without falling asleep. I had to keep waking him up to finish
chewing the mouthful of food he was on!

My family were no different. It had been exhausting for all of them
and very stressful, too. I had not realised just how much strain I had
put them under until the initial thrill was over and I stood back and
watched them one night. We had moved on to a nightclub on the edge
of the beach, which had a platform set back above the sand. I had been
so engrossed with talking to Russ and Amanda Corn on the platform
that I hadn't noticed what my family were doing. When I looked down
to the beach my family were all dancing maniacally – even my mother
and mother-in-law! They were all smiling, laughing and having a
wonderful time. They looked as though a load had been lifted from
their shoulders and they were thoroughly enjoying the weightlessness.

The following day a group of us jumped into cars and headed
towards the north of the island to take a look at North Point, the tip
of the island I had hoped to row around on the day I finished. As I
finished six miles north, I had not been able to see it and wanted to
see what I had missed. I had been told by Simon, of *UniS Voyager*,
that the woman who owned the café on North Point had been
following my progress. He suggested I should pop in and see her.

North Point is very dramatic. I watched the waves pounding the
jagged rocks and felt quite pleased I hadn't come too close! The
strong winds blowing off the Atlantic seemed so much more
threatening now that I was on dry land. We entered the small café to
shelter from the wind. The walls, bar and ceiling were covered in
business cards, some dating as far back as the 1960s. On the wall
next to the bar I noticed a familiar face – mine! Maritza, the owner,

really had been following my progress and had stuck newspaper clippings about me up on the wall.

'I'm so pleased you have come to see us,' she said in her unique Italian/Barbadian accent. 'We put up a big flag to welcome you in but we did not see you go by.'

I apologised, feeling sad to have disappointed her. 'I was too far north. The wind prevented me getting any closer.'

'Never mind. You are here now. We must put the flag back up.'

With that she was on the phone to her son, then off to her house to get it.

While we waited we took a tour of the Animal Flower Caves. The caves have been created by the power of the Atlantic waves driving against the cliff walls and the rock pools are full of beautiful 'flowers of the sea' – sea anemones. When we emerged from the caves, we noticed a huge white flag flying proudly from the old wooden flagpole on North Point. Sprayed in large red letters was the message WELCOME TO BARBADOS DEBORAH. Above it was a large Union flag and, above that, the flag of Barbados. I was overwhelmed by the effort they had taken to welcome me to their Island. It symbolised for me the kindness, warmth and friendly nature of all Barbadians I had met, none more so than my new friend Maritza.

Time alone with Andrew finally arrived, thanks to Tim and Jo of *Keltec Challenger*. When they had finished back in early December 2001, they celebrated at the fantastic Lone Star restaurant on Barbados. While there, they told the manager all about my solo voyage. They explained that I wouldn't be in for months, and that I was bound to be last. They built up an effective sob story to persuade the manager to give Andrew and me a free meal. Amazingly, he agreed and we were given a letter inviting us to dine courtesy of the Lone Star. With the sound of the ocean rolling in, great food and fantastic company, it was the perfect evening.

Towards the end of the meal a woman leaned across to our table from her own and said, 'I'm sorry to interrupt but do you mind if I ask you a question?'

Andrew immediately assumed that she wanted to ask if I was the woman who had just rowed the Atlantic and said, 'I know what you're going to ask!' Some confusion developed, as this hadn't been her intention, and the three of us were soon chuckling at the hole Andrew was digging himself into. At this point her husband joined in the conversation and as I turned to speak with him, I realised that he was the British actor Anthony Andrews, and this lovely, now rather confused lady, was his wife.

We soon shared our story with them, and they suggested ways to cope with the media attention. They even wrote down the name of a lawyer for me, should we need to consult a specialist in media. Just before they left the restaurant, Andrew asked, 'So what was it you were going to ask?' to which she replied, 'Well it's rather embarrassing, but I was going to ask what suntan lotion Debra uses to get such a glowing tan!'

Chapter 10

Coming Full Circle

Flying back to England always fills me with pride. There's something about looking out of the window at the green fields below. The big old oak trees with their branches, thick and sturdy, reaching wide – like a father, open-armed and ready to embrace.

As usual, I hadn't been able to sleep on the plane. We landed at Heathrow at 5.30 in the morning – and I felt awful. A team from the Troika office turned up in force to welcome us back. They probably felt how I must have looked. Having travelled to a hotel near Heathrow the night before, they had occupied the bar until just a few hours before our plane arrived. A huge banner had been produced, which read WELCOME HOME DEBRA AND ANDREW – but unfortunately the banner carrier had overslept. Russell looked more than a bit flustered as he ran in with it after we'd already been standing in arrivals for ten minutes! Poor Russell – it was a while before he lived that one down! We were so delighted to see them all. They had gone way above and beyond their sponsorship obligations.

The urban landscape I saw before me as I stepped out of the terminal building and the tropical one I had left behind in the Caribbean could not have been more different. The overcast English day seemed mottled and grey after the vibrancy of everything in

Barbados. It was as if the brightness, colour and contrast levels of the day had been turned right down. The picture of England before me was very much black and white, whereas every scene in Barbados had been like an exotic movie on a wide-screen colour TV. In England the air was filled with the smell of car fumes and pollution. The aroma of the ocean was sadly becoming a distant memory. But it was home.

Two hours later, a broadsheet newspaper journalist was interviewing us. To our amazement, far from the story being dead and buried after our two-week break in Barbados, it was very much still alive. Having a break from it after the initial media flurry in Barbados had given me time to reflect. I was a little more prepared and no longer felt completely like the new kid at school.

Unfortunately, the media were still running with the 'husband abandons wife' story. The papers were always going to tell the story their way, no matter what we said. But live TV gave us complete control over how we told the story. There was no clever editing. What we said was what the public would hear. There was something very reassuring about that.

I have read few of the many hundreds of column inches that were written about us and I'm not sure I will ever read any more. Although they have generally been very positive, feel-good articles about achieving against the odds, I still find that reading about myself is a peculiar experience.

The question remaining on everyone's lips was, 'How has the experience affected your relationship?' Most expected me to be angry with Andrew for 'abandoning' me and were amazed that his leaving the boat had not been an issue for us. The fact that he was left with no option did not lessen my respect for him. Giving up and admitting defeat is often a far harder thing to do.

Thankfully I am not alone in my views on his bravery. For every tabloid journalist or presenter who claimed Andrew had deserted me, there were vast numbers of people who demonstrated their support of his decision. I loved reading the emails from men praising Andrew for his bravery and telling stories of their own fears. He had allowed them to be vulnerable.

✉

Congratulations also to your husband for
being brave enough to admit and respond
to the fear he, so understandably,
encountered. Takes a hero, not a fool, to
have the courage to take the decision he
took. Brian and Dominique, Hertfordshire.

✉

The humour your husband showed in
handling what I thought were some cheap
and stupid shots by the host said a lot
about the strength of his character and
the relationship you have with each
other. It must be enormously difficult
for you both to talk to people who can't
understand what he went through.

   I took part in the first Round World
yacht race Chay Blyth organised in 1992.
On the first leg to Rio I experienced a
claustrophobic panic attack one night so
out of the blue and debilitating it would
have been impossible for me to continue
if it had carried on. Fortunately on a
large yacht with plenty of company and a
bit of room to walk about it passed and
didn't return. Your husband could not
move around or walk it off; it must have
been horrendous for him. I'm getting a
panic attack just thinking about it!
Anyway good luck to both of you.
Steve West
British Steel 11

✉

I must congratulate Andrew for attempting
something that seems an impossible task.
I believe that Debra deserves all the
praise she gets, but Andrew has not yet
gotten the praise that he deserves! As
they say, 'IT'S NOT THE WINNING, BUT THE
TAKING PART THAT COUNTS'.
Best Regards to both of you,
Gagandeep Singh Bhogal

✉

I was very impressed by Andrew's honesty
and clarity about his reasons not to
continue. I find it particularly
refreshing to hear a man being open about
his fears. He also did a fantastic job
of not being drawn into the way in which
the item was being introduced i.e. 'Man
abandons wife mid-Atlantic'. His support
and love for you as a strong and highly
capable individual were very clear.
With love from a foggy, grey Oxfordshire,
Matt Wallis

Rather than driving us apart, the experience had brought us closer
together. The more the press tried to divide us, the more united we
felt. As I watched Andrew speaking with such honesty and lucidity
about what had happened, I felt such respect and admiration for
him. He, in turn, was proud of what I had achieved and respected
me for having the courage to continue alone. That mutual respect
bound us tight. He had been there for me every stroke of the way
and, despite what the press wrote, we had in my mind rowed the
Atlantic very much together. His support, advice and encouragement had got me to Barbados.

Getting home on that first day and closing the door behind us was blissful. Sleeping in our own bed for the first time in nearly five months was even better. After a two-week holiday it is always great to get back to your own bed – but after five months it is heaven. Each night as I lay cuddled up to Andrew, snuggled under our thick duvet, I found myself trying to remember exactly what it was like lying alone in the darkness in my little cabin on *Troika Transatlantic*. I thought about the times I would strip off my drenched clothes and crawl into the cabin, exhausted after the twelfth hour of rowing. I imagined the routine of drying myself off and brushing aside the fish scales and salt crystals from the cushions. I tried to hear the sound of the waves breaking against the plywood walls as I held Woody tight to my chest.

I had spent 111 nights at sea this way, but once I was home I found it hard to believe I had done it. On the surface, everything back home seemed very familiar, but the reality was that our lives were now completely different. Cooking dinner in my kitchen seemed normal enough, almost as if I had never been away. But, almost as soon as I stepped outside the front door and into a public place, the reality of my new life hit me. As I stood at the bank cash dispenser, people stopped to ask me if I was the woman who had just rowed the Atlantic. I would reach for vegetables in the supermarket, hear muffled whispers and then be asked for my autograph. I always love to share my experience of the ocean with people, so inevitably end up talking for ages. Consequently, shopping takes me much longer these days!

Being recognised in the media, or on the street, can be a very positive experience. The positives certainly outweighed the negatives for us. By telling the story openly and truthfully we hoped at best to inspire people or, if nothing else, put the record straight. We do hear or read negative profiles about ourselves, and often feel under pressure at having been thrust so swiftly into the public eye. But at those times we return to the positive emails and text messages we have been sent. They help us to put it all back into perspective.

✉

Two years ago, aged 34, I had a heart and lung transplant as the lungs I grew up with had been buggered up by Cystic Fibrosis. I vowed that I would try to do something extraordinary with my life. I tell you this for no other reason than I have been so inspired and deeply moved by your achievement – it certainly puts my Zambezi idea in the shade! More than you will ever know, you have had a profound impact upon many people. For me, it has lifted my spirits at a difficult time and reminded me how important it is to persevere, even against the odds. Thank you for that.
Martin Wragg, Grimsby, UK

✉

Dear Andrew and Debra
I wanted to reach out to you after seeing you on J. Vaughan last night . . . what an inspiration. I cried witnessing your love for each other, an inspiration which also touched a deep sadness in me as my partner recently moved out. We are still together, there's a lot of love between us, but we were not functioning well as a family living together – I have an 11yr old son and he and Val struggled in their relationship. I see the love and the possibilities for us and sometimes it's hard to have faith. That's what you fuelled in me last night – faith, not in any religious way but faith in love and

how it can be between two people. You
were the stars last night (much that I
love Meg!), both of you. I'm sure you are
that for many who are fortunate to share
your lives.
Thank you :-)
Robin

But sometimes it is also nice not to be noticed. As I travelled into London on the train the week after our return, the woman opposite me was reading a broadsheet containing a feature about me. I waited as she slowly thumbed the pages, expecting her to do a 'double take' and begin the questions any minute. As she turned to page 11, a large close-up photograph of my face stared up at her from the page. I noticed that I had my hair in exactly the same style and was wearing the same yellow jacket that morning as featured in the photograph. I still found it surreal to see my face staring out at me from the pages of a national newspaper.

I watched as the woman paused over the page and proceeded to read the whole article. At the end she looked up and straight at me. But there was not even a flicker of recognition.

As the number of newspaper, TV and radio interviews began to reduce, I was recognised less often. It had been frantic at first. One day I squeezed in three TV programmes and a photo shoot. It made me appreciate how hard worldwide promotional work for albums and films must be. I worked only on a small scale and for a relatively short period, but it was difficult to keep producing creative and interesting answers.

Between interviews, I set myself a personal goal: to reply to everyone who had sent me an email of encouragement. Most were from supporters I have never met, but their words had been vital. It was important to me to write and thank each of them personally. I had over a thousand replies to write. It was an enormously time-consuming task, but worth it.

As I worked my way through the inbox, I was overjoyed to

discover an email from Nikki and Pete, the British couple from *Seventh Heaven* who had kindly given me some bread and biscuits mid-Atlantic. They were still in the Caribbean but had managed to track down the *Troika Transatlantic* website while I was still at sea. I had been so annoyed with myself for not having taken down an email address for them, so it was a great surprise to see the email that they had sent some weeks before my finish. Perhaps we'll meet again one day – in the mid-Atlantic, or the UK.

> Hi. We met Debra in the middle of the Atlantic a couple of weeks ago or more on our way to Barbados. We have a couple of photos, which we'd be happy to send on to any relatives if they'd like. All in all she looked very well and was doubly excited to speak English, all be it very brief. Please pass on our details to her on her return.
> Thanks and regards
> Pete and Nikki (Crew of Seventh Heaven)

It was also great to hear from two members of the *Wild Woman* crew who had sailed past me without noticing, until I called them on the VHF radio.

> Since nearly running you down mid-way across we have thought many times of the weird things that you pass, e.g. plastic bottles, jerry cans, bits of fishing net and other flotsam but I never expected to pass a solo rower. Also though our offers of assistance were turned down – have joked that you were lucky to meet

us when you did as a week later into our
trip and I may have had trouble
controlling the rest of the 'Wild
Womanisers' (the sea does do strange
things to people).
Congratulations on your arrival and your
perseverance sets a shining example to
all of us who set out to sea.
All the best,
Fred

✉

I was aboard the sailing yacht Wild Woman
along with 4 other crewmembers who looked
in astonishment and disbelief as we
sailed by. Involving my self in my first
transatlantic crossing, which I
considered to be the most incredible
experience of my life, with 4 other lads,
and a boat 3 times the size as your small
dodgem car. It made me realise what guts,
determination and a strong minded person
is able to achieve. Well done for
completing your goal and thank you for
the inspiration that you gave out to me
and everyone else.
Yours sincerely
John Jones (Australian).

With the emails all replied to, I set about meeting new opportunities
I'd been given as a consequence of the voyage. Somehow I needed to
make them fit into my pre-Atlantic life.

Before I had left England in September, life had been full of The
Well Hung Art Company. Now there were a whole host of speaking
engagements, charity work, planning for new adventures, and the

possibility of a new job in television to be considered. I was back to living life at a hundred miles per hour, quite the opposite of the peaceful and tranquil life I had found on the ocean.

I sometimes catch myself dreaming about the cool sea air on my skin and the deadly silence of a calm Atlantic day as I put on a smart suit and head into London on a hot and crowded tube. I wouldn't say one is better than the other. Perhaps it's the combination of the two extremes that keeps life interesting.

The diversity reached its extreme when I was invited to be one of seven guests of honour at a dinner being given by the Duke of Edinburgh's Award. It meant joining the Earl and Countess of Wessex on the top table.

The 'Magnificent 7' was a fundraising event held to honour seven people who had recently achieved something magnificent. It has to be said that I felt completely out of touch, as I had been away during the period in which the other six guests were doing whatever it was they did magnificently.

I was really quite worried when I was informed that a young man named Will Young would also be on our table. I had been told that he had won an incredibly popular TV talent show called *Pop Idol*, which everyone seemed to have heard about except me. I had no idea what he looked like, less about how he sang, so I was quite relieved when he pulled out at the last moment. No doubt I would otherwise have made a fool of myself by asking him why he was magnificent!

In preparation for the evening, I rushed into town to buy a new dress. Perhaps not looking my smartest, in track pants and trainers, I entered an exclusive dress shop. They stocked the latest designer dresses, but the atmosphere was that of an old-fashioned tailor. A mature lady eyed me suspiciously over the top of her half-moon glasses. She probably expected me to head straight for the sale rail, or help myself and run. I wandered around the shop, her eyes following me, burning a hole in my back. Finally, she joined me reluctantly and asked what I was looking for and whether I would like any help. I smiled sweetly and answered, 'I'm looking for an evening dress'. She looked first disbelieving, then bored, and asked

'Is it for a special occasion?' I told her it was.

There was something about the way she spoke that made me feel I was wasting her time. As if she wanted to catch me out, the questions continued.

'Are you going anywhere nice?'

I wasn't intending to tell her, but mischievously, and perhaps because I could anticipate the response, I casually mentioned that I was having dinner with Prince Edward and his wife.

It was like flicking a switch.

Immediately I became the most important person in the shop. She hurried around the rails, pulling out dresses and holding them up against me as if her life depended on my immaculate turnout and fearing she'd be sent to the tower if I had an inch of silk out of place.

I found it hard to keep the grin off my face. I felt just like Julia Roberts shopping in *Pretty Woman* and left the shop swinging the bag – containing my elegant new evening dress – in much the same way.

Towards the end of March, after a month of being back in the UK, Tim from *Keltec Challenger* organised an Atlantic Rowers' Reunion one Friday night in London. I still owed Tim and Jo a meal after their fantastic singing and my poor joke-telling and could not wait to see them, and the rest of the rowers. Unfortunately, only one other rower, Graham from the *George Geary*, had made it. I was really disappointed. But it was indicative, I suppose, of the fact that they had all been back for many months and were caught up in the humdrum of daily life once again.

Tim and Jo were on fine form, as always, even if there was a distinct lack of joke-telling and singing! We had all moved on. Tim had got engaged to the lovely Rebecca and Jo was back to his PE teaching and rugby playing, and preparing to run the London Marathon. But we shared stories of our best and the worst moments at sea, and lots of sympathy about bottom sores! And these were mine:

My Top Ten Worst Memories

10. The day I had beef stew and dumplings for the fifth day in a row.

9. Day 93 – when I woke to find almost forty dead flying fish on the boat. I normally found only about ten at the most. The stench was overpowering.

8. Day 91 – Splashback from the poo bucket. As I threw the contents overboard, they splashed back into my face and into my mouth. Much spitting and rubbing with baby wet wipes followed.

7. Night of Day 89 – When an oar broke free while still in its gate, and wrapped itself under the boat. Fighting with the oar as the waves broke over me was not a good night out!

6. Day 85 – Between Christmas and New Year – in my diary I wrote, 'I feel so worn down. Every time I look out of the hatch at the ocean I feel so trapped because I know I can't give up.' I got myself so worked up about having to spend another four weeks alone that I was inconsolable for much of the afternoon.

5. Day 19 – A shark swam under the boat that night, chasing fish. I watched the trail of glowing phosphorescence as it shot through the water at high speeds and convinced myself that it was going to attack the boat, so I hid in the cabin, very scared, until dawn.

4. Day 14 – The day Andrew left the boat. I couldn't help thinking that if anything went wrong we might never see each other again.

3. Ten days of unbearable loneliness at the start of December, which climaxed on Day 65 when I cried from 8 a.m. till 11 a.m., until I finally found enough strength to get out of the cabin and row.

2. Day 23 – Everything seemed to be going wrong, then I nearly got run down by a supertanker. I was at an all-time low.

1. Day 8 – Disastrous day for a very unhappy Andrew. It culminated in a thunder-and-lightning storm with driving rain and, having completed a double night shift, I found Andrew in the cabin curled up, shaking and unable even to talk to me.

My Top Ten Best Memories

10. Day 6 – First night rowing with the stars out. It was breathtakingly beautiful as I watched dozens of shooting stars trailing across the night sky.

9. Day 64 – After an emotional day crying at the oars, I was looking for the rice and found a whole bag of thirty Pepperamis and thirty packs of Minstrels that I had forgotten.

8. Day 74 – Having not seen anyone for a month, I crossed sea paths with a yacht called *Seventh Heaven*, whose crew gave me a loaf of fresh bread, some awesome chocolate biscuits and, more importantly, ten minutes of talking face to face with other humans.

7. Day 76 – When I secretly arranged to talk via speakerphone to all the Troika staff while they were in a company meeting just before Christmas.

6. Day 54 – First day of surfing really big waves. It was awesome (and risky) – my grin was so big, you could have hooked the corners of my mouth over my ears.

5. Day 24 – The day I spent with Albert the turtle while he ate weed off the hull.

4. Day 75 – Being surrounded by playful dolphins, who were diving and doing somersaults right in front of me.

3. Christmas Day – Reading all my Christmas cards from my friends and family in the UK.

2. Day 4 – Rowing at 3 a.m. with Andrew, laughing and singing 'Jerusalem' and 'I Vow to Thee My Country' at the top of our voices to keep ourselves awake.

1. Day 21 – Watching the most beautiful sunrise and feeling all the pain and anguish over my father's death fade away, leaving me inspired and crying tears of happiness.

Easter weekend 2002 fell on the last week of March. Andrew and I returned to Devon together for the first time since the previous year. It was the longest period I had spent without a visit to my mum's house. Mum had moved from Rose Cottage to a smaller house in the next-door village after Dad had died. It is a house I really don't know. I still have to open every cupboard door in the kitchen when looking for a plate to use. The people are familiar but the place isn't. I miss Rose Cottage – it holds so many special memories for me, and for all of us – but Mum had been right to move on.

It's always been rare for us to get all the members of our family together to share a big Sunday roast, but we managed it – almost – that Easter Sunday. When we were growing up, Mum and Dad attached great importance to having a big family meal together every Sunday. I loved those special meals. When I was young, Matt would always crack jokes and make me giggle at the table. He'd time his delivery to coincide perfectly with my taking a mouthful of drink, because he knew if he made me laugh hard enough the drink would come out of my nose! As I watched Matt at the table that Sunday, it seemed that we had stepped back in time. Nothing had changed – except that one very important person was missing from the head of the table. I had found mealtimes uncomfortable in the early days after Dad's death, but they had become easier. I was once again able to smile at the memory of him saying, 'Well that was a gastronomic delight!' at the end of the meal.

On Easter Monday Andrew and I drove past Rose Cottage and through the village up to the church. The cottage looked a bit unloved and unlived in, as it had been empty until quite recently. I shut my eyes and tried to remember it as it had been – a loving, warm family home. As we pulled up in the church car park, the drizzle was running down the windows. Outside the car seemed like a very uninviting place to be, but I'd been looking forward to visiting Dad's grave to tell him about my adventures for some time. A little bit of rain wasn't going to hold me back. After all, I'd been soggier.

As we walked around to the graveyard on the far side of the church, the wet grass quickly soaked through my shoes, making my toes tingle. It had been cut for Easter weekend and the clumps of cuttings stuck to our shoes as we walked. The countryside surrounding us smelled wonderful. Poking my head out from under my tiny umbrella, I could hear birds singing cheerfully, blocking out the dreary noise of the rain pitter-pattering on to the canvas. The Devonshire countryside bordering the church was being washed a brighter, fresher green by the shower. To one side in a field, a herd of cows stood watching us with mild curiosity. Behind a fence on the other, a solitary horse looked less than impressed with the weather conditions. We were only a few miles from the coast of Torbay, and a few seagulls had ventured inland and were flying overhead. They somehow seemed symbolic. Despite the rain, Dad's resting place was as beautiful as I'd remembered it.

His grave, however, looked completely different. It had been over half a year since I had been to Devon and in that time the grave had settled. The ground was no longer bumpy and uneven, but flat like the graves that were decades old.

'Oh – it looks really different.' I wasn't really saying the words to Andrew, more observing aloud to myself.

'Does it?' Andrew asked. He was getting quite wet standing by the grave, unable to fit under the one tiny umbrella we had found in the car.

'Yes, the ground's settled or something.'

My disjointed comments could have been designed to hide my fragility. We stood in silence for a few minutes, staring at the headstone.

'You're getting soaked,' I said to Andrew. 'Do you want to go and wait in the car?'

'Why, is this going to take some time?' he asked. His face was full of concern and understanding.

'Well, if it's OK, I'd just like to stay a while and talk to Dad.'

Andrew smiled and kissed me on the forehead. 'Of course,' he replied gently, and turned to walk back to the car.

I realised Dad, the real Dad I knew and loved, was somewhere much more wonderful than that pretty churchyard. I felt sure I would see him again one day. But, just for now, this seemed a good place to come and talk. I crouched down next to the gravestone, curling up under the umbrella and sitting back on my haunches.

'Hi, Dad, it's me. I'm back. I've been on the most amazing adventure. I've come to tell you all about it.' I hadn't really thought about what I wanted to say. I didn't need to. Story after story of the highs and lows of my adventure came flooding out. I described *Troika* in all her glory. I told him about Mum and the rest of the family coming to Barbados and how it had brought us all together, and I explained how I had made peace with the knowledge that he was no longer on earth.

'Anyway, Dad, I wanted to come here today to thank you. I would have never made it without you. Whenever I felt like giving up, I thought of your journey with cancer and how you never gave up on your dream of retiring to *Rio Luna* and cruising around the Med with Mum. You hadn't given up on your dream, so there was no way I could give up on mine. You taught me through your actions. You taught me what it means to believe.'

I paused.

'Dad, I wanted to leave a piece of my boat with you. You've given me so much in my life that made my voyage possible. You taught me I could live my dreams. I have, and I will. I just wanted to share them with you.'

I pulled a small metal shackle from my pocket. I had removed it from *Troika Transatlantic* after the finish for this very purpose. 'Here, this is for you.' I said, and pushed the shackle deep into the damp earth at the base of Dad's headstone.

Then I pulled myself to my feet, and wiping my eyes on the back of my hand, I whispered, 'Bye, Dad.' And walked back the way I had come, to be with Andrew.

Epilogue

Andrew's diary update – Easter 2002

So, in a sense, the journey's over. Now that Debra has been back to her father's grave, one thread of the story which became more significant than we ever imagined has reached a natural conclusion.

Do I regret the way it all turned out?

How can I, when almost everything that has come of it has been good? The doors which have opened are many and various and the people we have met, together and individually, have been variously kind, interesting and inspirational.

In so many other ways, though, there is no end to this journey for either of us, as life will never be quite the same again.

I was very disappointed initially. A lot of time, effort and money had gone towards our aim to row across the Atlantic together – and it didn't happen. It was also one of the only times I had ever really tried to do something and failed.

But, as the disappointment faded, I started to look at the adventure over three-and-a-half years instead of three-and-a-half months. During that time we managed to be one of only 35 boats (out of more than 70 which entered at various stages) to beg, borrow and raise enough money to get to the start with a boat that was capable of making the trip. The whole experience has taught us a lot about ourselves, and each other and brought us closer together. We discovered a combination of skills between us which made it all possible and the mindset brought about by being a part of the adventure caused us both to make some significant life changes before we even started.

In my case, after years of working for big companies, I tried working for two small ones, both of which worked out really badly. Then I came across Troika, much smaller, at that time, than the preceding two and it has worked out brilliantly.

In Debra's case, teaching gave way to an art company, to which have now been added opportunities for inspirational public speaking and the possibility of a career making TV documentaries.

Things don't always have to work out as planned, to work out well. Had everything gone according to plan, it would have taken us years to pay off the money we borrowed and the rowing would have been our one big adventure. Now we find ourselves facing a number of other possibilities and a situation where raising backing for another trip is likely to be far more straightforward. Suddenly, a number of things I never thought I would do are possible – ballooning round the world, competing in the Paris–Dakar rally, who knows what else?

Occasionally people ask why would I risk doing something else and the possibility (hopefully remote!) of not making it again. Obviously, it was a bit embarrassing for a while. There are always people who want to knock you, for a number of reasons, but you realise in the end that they are either trying to sell papers, are jealous or they didn't like you anyway, so what does it matter? Hopefully, even in reading this book, some of the journalists who made assumptions or made stuff up are feeling mildly foolish themselves. Don't suppose they'll make a headline out of it, though!

As we used to say occasionally to people who asked why we wanted to row across the Atlantic, 'If you have to ask the question, you won't understand the answer.'

It's not about becoming famous and it's certainly not about what other people think. It's about having one life and trying to make the most of it. Perhaps it doesn't matter what dream you pursue – the chances are something different will happen anyway.

The journey is only just beginning.

'Adventure is worthwhile in itself' – Amelia Earhart

Glossary

Antifoul Paintlike covering applied to the hull of a boat, intended to discourage the growth of algae and barnacles. Proved not to be completely turtle-proof.

Bow The front end of the boat.

Broach When a boat turns side-on to the waves.

Bulkhead Any upright wall-like partition in a boat, built to hold back water.

Challenge Business Company formed by Sir Chay Blyth. Organisers of the Ward Evans Atlantic Rowing Challenge and the only wrong-way-round-the-world yacht race – known in recent years as the BT Global Challenge.

Challenge support yachts Two yachts, numbers 24 and 47, formerly used in the BT Global Challenge, that remained in the Atlantic, moving among the crews throughout the course of the race.

Cleat Device fixed to a boat, used to attach lines or ropes. Usually in the shape of two prongs sticking out from a central base.

Drogue Device shaped like a small parachute, deployed underwater at the end of a rope from either the bow or stern of a boat to decrease speed and/or increase stability in rough seas.

Double scull Rowing boat for two people, using two oars (known as sculls) each.

EPIRB Emergency Position Indicating Radio Beacon. Device used to notify international rescue services if a vessel is in distress via a global satellite network.

Ergometer Exercise equipment, which simulates the action of rowing (on perfectly flat water), used in training by rowers.

Foot well Lower areas of the deck, one inside and one outside the hatch, into the cabin. As it turned out, a good place to store the life raft.

GPS   Global Positioning System. A network of satellites, owned by the US military, which is capable of pinpointing a receiving device to within six feet anywhere on the earth's surface. Considerably easier than a sextant. There was some danger that the system might be switched off for commercial use, if the US went to war at the end of 2001. Thankfully for all concerned, that didn't happen, but we had a sextant on board just in case.

GPS screen   Display fitted to the boat to show position and course, transmitted from the GPS satellites. Also capable of being programmed with a number of predetermined waypoints to enable checking against a planned course.

Gunwale   Horizontal side panels, higher than and running the length of the deck. Used to support the rowing gates through which the oars pivot.

Inmarsat-D   A device used to transmit a boat's position. Compulsory for boats in the rowing race, which can then be contacted (polled) from race headquarters to establish their precise position at any time. Used by the race organisers to update positions on the race website. Proved to be quite a drain on power, so crews tended not to keep them on all the time.

Jackstays   Cables running the length of the deck, to which it was possible to clip a lifejacket or harness, and therefore avoid being thrown overboard in rough seas.

Nautical mile   Unit of distance used in navigation. Defined as equal to one degree of latitude over the earth's surface, which is equivalent to 1,852 metres or 1.15 miles. Close to the equator, also nearly the same as one degree of longitude over the earth's surface.

Oar gate   More commonly known as an oarlock or rowlock, the oar gate is a hard plastic square through which the oar passes. The oar gate creates a fulcrum and a collar on the oar prevents the oar from sliding out of the boat.

Para-anchor   A parachute-like device deployed just under the surface of the water, similar to a drogue. The para-anchor is particularly effective in countering backwards movement of an Atlantic rowing boat in strong winds.

Polling   See Inmarsat-D above.

Port   The left side of the vessel when facing the bow.

Scuppers   Holes in the side of the boat at deck level to allow water to drain out. *Troika*'s started out with flexible plastic covers so they didn't also let water in just as readily. As the deck is open to the elements, the covers were an optional extra, and some of them came off in the big waves.

Shackle   A U-shaped metal fastening used on board *Troika Transatlantic* to attach the safety lines to the boat.

Sikkaflex   Stickiest substance in the world, completely irremovable from skin and clothing. Used as a sealant in the construction of boats.

Starboard   The right side of a vessel when facing the bow.

Stern   The rear part of the boat.

Sudacrem   A soothing cream and a particularly effective treatment for nappy rash. Don't put to sea without it!

Tender   Small vessel kept aboard or attached to a larger one, used to ferry people and material to and from shore and other boats. In the case of the Challenge yachts, small inflatable dinghies.

Trimming the boat   To store food and heavy items in the hull of the rowing boat and lockers to achieve even weight distribution so that the boat does not list to one side or the other. As I became more familiar with how *Troika Transatlantic* behaved in certain wave or weather conditions, I was able to trim the boat (move the weight around) to achieve better speed or stability. For example, in a large swell I would move all heavy items, including the life raft, into the main cabin at the back of the boat and lighten the bow. This would help *Troika Transatlantic* maintain a straight course down the front of large waves.

VHF   Abbreviation for Very High Frequency radio.

Appendix

Troika Transatlantic and the origins of the Atlantic Rowing Boat

Renowned boat builders and designers Peter 'Spud' Rowsell and Philip Morrison received their brief from Sir Chay Blyth CBE BEM: *to design a rowing boat capable of undertaking a competitively rowed ocean passage, to accommodate two people with their stores and allow simple construction worldwide.*

Atlantic Rowing Challenge Class of Boat

BOAT DESIGNERS	Phil Morrison & Peter 'Spud' Rowsell	
KIT DESIGNER	Jim Moore	
LENGTH	7.1 metres	23.4 feet
BEAM	1.9 metres	6.3 feet
WEIGHT – FULLY LADEN	750 kg	1,650 lbs
BUILD INFORMATION	Made from marine plywood and supplied in laser cut kits	
NUMBER OF CREW	2	

Since 1995 when the first Atlantic Rowing Challenge class boat was launched, 62 Atlantic Rowing Challenge boats have been produced. The Atlantic Rowing Challenge class boat has now successfully

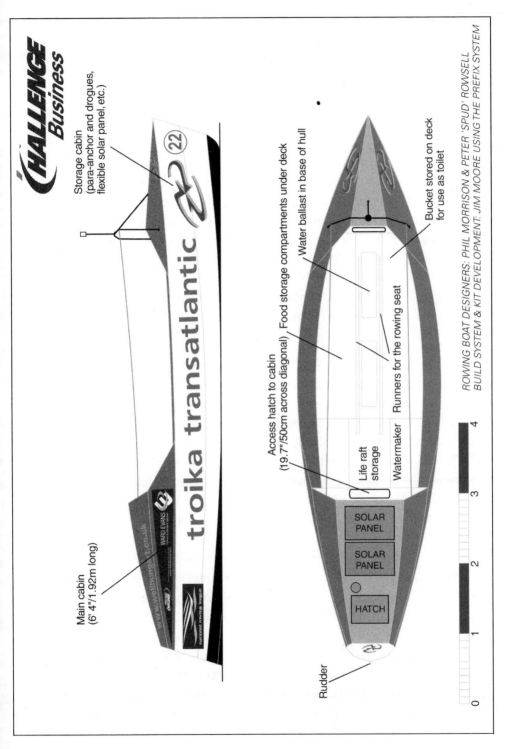

Storage cabin (para-anchor and drogues, flexible solar panel, etc.)

Main cabin (6' 4"/1.92m long)

troika transatlantic

CHALLENGE *Business*

Access hatch to cabin (19.7"/50cm across diagonal)

Food storage compartments under deck

Water ballast in base of hull

Bucket stored on deck for use as toilet

Life raft storage

Watermaker

Runners for the rowing seat

SOLAR PANEL

SOLAR PANEL

HATCH

Rudder

ROWING BOAT DESIGNERS: PHIL MORRISON & PETER 'SPUD' ROWSELL BUILD SYSTEM & KIT DEVELOPMENT: JIM MOORE USING THE PREFIX SYSTEM

Illustration by Sally Kiff

crossed an ocean 62 times (57 of these as part of the Atlantic Rowing Challenge event), making it far and away the most successful design of Ocean Rowing boat in the world.

For safety the boat is extensively subdivided into watertight compartments and the disposition of the aft accommodation and forward stowage, together with the raised double bottom, ensures that the boat is fully self-righting and will be largely self-draining.

The boat consists of a larger rear cabin where the rowers sleep and shelter in severe weather conditions. This measures just 6ft 4in at the longest part. The middle section of the boat comprises an open deck with a forward stowage compartment at the bow.

Troika Transatlantic: 24 sheets of laser-cut marine ply + lots of epoxy = one Atlantic rowing boat

As part of Sir Chay Blyth's goal to make the race as equal as possible, all competitors in the Ward Evans Atlantic Rowing Race had to use the same design of rowing boat. Each boat arrived as a flat-packed kit comprising 24 sheets of laser-cut marine ply. It was then up to each team to organise the building and fitting-out of their own boat. It's all part of the challenge. Some teams chose to build the boat themselves, often having no other option with finances being limited. *Troika Transatlantic* had her basic structure built by Rossiter Yachts in Christchurch, Dorset, but had the fittings and finishing touches completed by Stanley & Thomas Boat Builders in Windsor.

One of the questions that I frequently get asked is, 'Where do you go to the toilet?'. The boats have an open deck platform where the rowing takes place and one small cabin in the aft, but no toilet! I used a bucket-and-chuck-it system on deck – the most scenic toilet I have ever used.

I used two rigid and two flexible solar panels to power the watermaker, GPS, satellite phone, navigation light and Inmarsat D terminal, which tracked my position. The food was packed into the hull, under the rowing positions and was cooked on a small gas stove.

The financial cost of rowing the Atlantic

Item	Approx. Cost in £ Sterling
Ward Evans Atlantic Rowing Challenge race registration and entry fee	13,800
Hire of the hull from original owners	4,500
Boat Builders' fees from cleats to moulded rowing seats (materials and labour)	18,000
Compulsory race electronics: solar panels, GPS, VHF, batteries, etc., plus electrical instillation costs	9,000
Racing oars and spares, etc,	1,800
Compulsory race equipment: water-maker, cooker, etc,	2,500
Compulsory safety equipment: life raft, life jackets, etc.	1,900
Food and supplements for 70 days × 2 people	1,000
Boat trailer	1,800
Branding and painting the hull	3,000
Medical kit	300
Shipping the boat to Tenerife and back from Barbados	4,000
Cushions for cabin, canvas oar end holders and canvas covers	1,000
Satellite phone and phone bill	12,500
Insurance	1,000

Flights and accommodation pre- and post-race	4,000
Branded team clothing	2,000
Training – gym membership, sea trials, boat hire, etc.	1,000
Courses – Tideway Sculler School, Ocean Navigation, Sea Survival, VHF, etc.	700
TOTAL COST	83,800

In addition to sponsorship provided by Troika UK Ltd, some of the costs listed above were kindly absorbed by sponsors and we would particularly like to thank the following:

Challenge Business International Ltd
Ocean Safety
XM Yachting
Garmin
Musto Ltd
Science in Sport
Thomas and Cath Herbert

Medical Kit taken on board Troika Transatlantic

ANALGESICS FOR PAIN
Coproxamol Tab × 100 only
Dihydrocodiene × 30
Brufen 400mg × 100 Tablets
Oruvail Gel 100g tube
Aspirin 300mg × 32
Deep Heat Spray 150 gsm

ANTIBIOTICS FOR INFECTION
Augmentin 375mg Tabs × 21
Erythromycin 250mgm Tabs × 28

Ciproxin Ciprofloxacin 500mg × 20
400mg tablets/Flagyl × 14
Flucloxacilin 250mg capsules × 28
Trimethoprim tablets 200mg × 14
Cicatrin powder 50gm each

ACUTE ANXIETY/FITS
Diazepam tablets 5mg × 30

DRESSINGS
Various crepe bandages and dressings
Zinc Oxide 7.5 × 5m
Jelonet 10cm × 10cm
Cotton wool 25g in mini-grip bags
Elastoplast adhesive bandage
Micropore 2.5cm × 9.2 cm × 2

EARS AND EYES
Neo-Cortef 1.5% (Eye/ear – Drops)
0.3% Hypromellose
Chloramphenicol eye ointment 1%
Optrex with eye bath
Amethocaine Minims 0.5%
Fluorescein Fluorets

NOSE AND MOUTH
Karvol capsules
Ephedrine nasal drops 1%
Strepsils
Adcortyl Orabase

ALLERGY/ASTHMA/ANAPHYLAXIS
Piriton 4mg × 30
Prednisolone 5mg tablets × 28
Hydrocortisone 100mg (Solu-Cortef)

Adrenaline injection 1:1000
Various syringes and needles

STOMACH AND GUT
Gaviscon tablets × 48
Imodium capsules
Dioralyte EFF tablets – 10's
Anusol Suppositories – 12's
Glycerin suppositories – constipation 4g

SKIN PREPARATIONS
Calamine lotion – (Plastic Bottles × 2)
E45 cream 50 kg × 2
Sudocrem (nappy rash cream!)
Zovirax 2 kg × 2
Flamazine 50 g × 2
Hydrocortisone cream 0.5% – 15g
Vaseline/Petroleum Jelly
Tisept
Ster-Zac powder
Daktarin cream and powder

CARDIAC PACK
Glyceryl Trintrate spray (Nitrolingual)

ANAESTHETICS
Emla cream 2 × 5g

HARDWARE
Large Medicut chest
Gloves (sterile latex size medium)
Tuff Cut scissors
Disposable scalpel (sterile)
Various sized threads
4mm × 76mm Leukostrip/Steristrip

Foil blanket
5-inch SH/SH scissors
Safety pins
Clinical thermometer
Magnifying glass – small
Toothed forceps gillies
Spencer Wells Artery Forceps: curved and straight
Sam splint
Pen torch with batteries
Cotton buds

For us, the Diazepam tablets were the most useful part of the first aid kit. Andrew took them to help control his anxieties and initially they worked well. I used very little of the first-aid kit but it was reassuring to have. Instead of being seasick for the first week, I had severe indigestion. I have no idea why the motion of the ocean caused it, but the Gaviscon tablets helped ease the burning pain. I also used the Sudocrem, Vaseline and E45 to control any skin irritations – mainly on my bottom from hours of sitting on the rowing seat!

Other than that, I mostly used the elements of the first-aid kit for duties other than what they were designed for. In particular, the various crepe bandages and dressings were a brilliant substitute for toilet paper after I had run out of the standard variety.

Extracts from my diary:

Top 10 weird things about not being on this boat any more:

10. Coping with an English winter after having spent 4 months in temperatures over 30°C.

9. Being able to have a lie-in rather than getting up at 5.30 a.m. to row.

8. Not having to repeatedly get up in the night to look for supertankers.

7. Inevitably getting drunk on one sniff of a rum cocktail.

6. Eating – my digestive system is not functioning well after 3½ months of processed slop.

5. Going to the toilet indoors (I'll miss the view of an open-air pooh!).

4. Sleeping in a bed that doesn't move.

3. Being surrounded by people and having no time to myself.

2. Wearing clothes and shoes again.

1. Walking on dry land – apparently it's impossible to walk without swaying.

Top 10 favourite rowing the Atlantic songs

Before I left the UK, Tony Humpreys at the Challenge Business told me that when he sailed the Atlantic he ended up listening to his mellower music more than anything else. He was right. I found the same. Life at sea is so simple and chilled out that nothing else seems appropriate. This top 10 was by far the hardest to write. I managed to shortlist 25 songs and it then took ages to whittle it down to the following top 10.

10. 'Givin' up'/'Worth it' – Harry Diamond/Skinny (Ministry Chillout session 2)

9. 'You get what you give' – New Radicals

8. 'Achilles Heel' – Toploader

7. 'Drops of Jupiter' – Train

6. 'Mr. Jones' – Counting Crows

5. The whole of the 'Funk Odyssey' album – Jamiroquai

4. 'Street Spirit' – Radiohead

3. 'Demons' – Fat Boy Slim feat. Macy Gray

2. 'Moon River' – version by Danny Williams

1. 'Dream a little dream' – Mama Cass

Top Ten Next Big Challenges

Just before I arrived in Barbados I put out a call on my website asking supporters to text me their suggestions for my next big challenge. After a weekend of high drama, these suggestions helped restore my sense of humour.

10. Fatty Arbuckle's Challenge – Eat 50 ounces (-ish) of steak and get the whole of your party's meal for free. Now that really would be a challenge after over 100 days on freeze-dried slop! (From Caroline at Appeal PR)

 9. Inspire 120 people to challenge themselves to go far beyond their perceived limits as you have done. (From Chuck Wilson in Palow Alto, CA)

 8. Literally right in the middle of Ireland geographically speaking, is Lough Dearg. Row round it and you will have rowed round Ireland. (From Matt Jess)

 7. Visit every state in the USA in a month. (From Michelle at Appeal PR) – This would have been right at the top of the list if it suggested I should attempt to kayak a river in every state within a month.

 6. Walk the Great Wall of China. (From Sue, Mum of Helen at Hemsley Fraser Training Group Ltd)

 5. Three-in-one Challenge – climb a mountain, dive a lake, trek a jungle. (From Emma Cunningham)

 4. Learn to ride a motorbike and ride around the world. (From Emma Cunningham) I once watched a programme about a guy who did this. I'm not sure if this challenge has been completed by a woman yet.

 3. Be the first person to row round the three great Capes: go down

to Cape Horn – row round it. Go to Western Australia – row round Cape Leewin. Go to Cape Town – row round the Cape of Good Hope. You wouldn't have to worry about the bits in the middle, like oceans! (From Matt Jess)

2. Bicycle the parameter of the Mediterranean. (From Eliza in New York).

1. High altitude jump from the outer edges of space. 150,000 feet approximately. Don a space suite and go for the female record. Any height over 100,000 feet would do. (From Tim in Ireland)

The Times believed this final suggestion. On Monday 29 January the headline on the front page of *The Times* read: 'Now sky's the limit for Debra lone Atlantic rower.' They wrote: 'Debra Veal . . . has set herself a new challenge – jumping to earth form the edge of space.' Within hours of the headline being published we received an email from Cameron Balloons (of Breitling Orbiter 3 fame) stating that they could make the balloon to get me up there!

Things I wouldn't set out to sea in a rowing boat without

Sense of humour
Satellite phone
Music
Pen and paper
GPS, chart and compass
Para-anchor
Woody (the ship's bear)

I wish I had taken

More toilet rolls
A wider variety of main meals
A better steering system
Water bottles that had lids
Food with longer 'Best Before' dates

Pages from my logbook

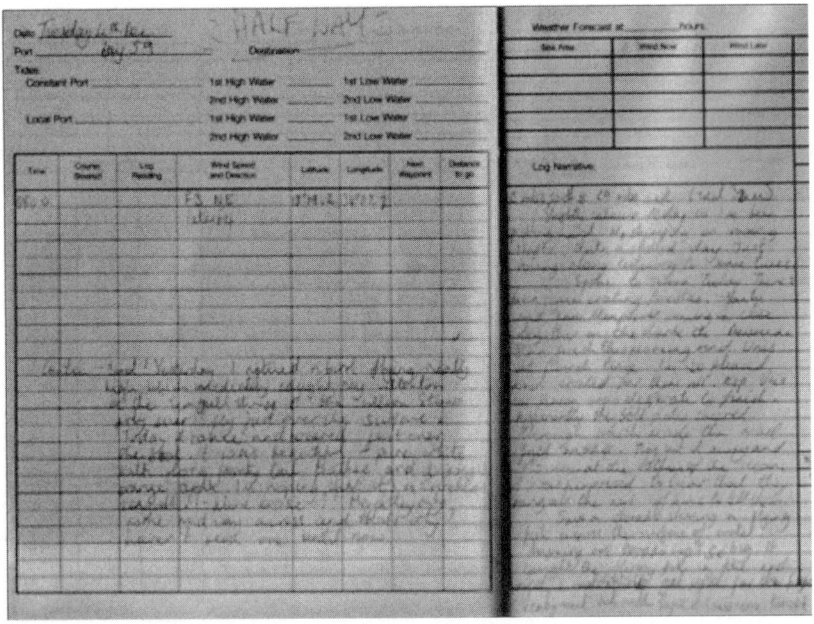

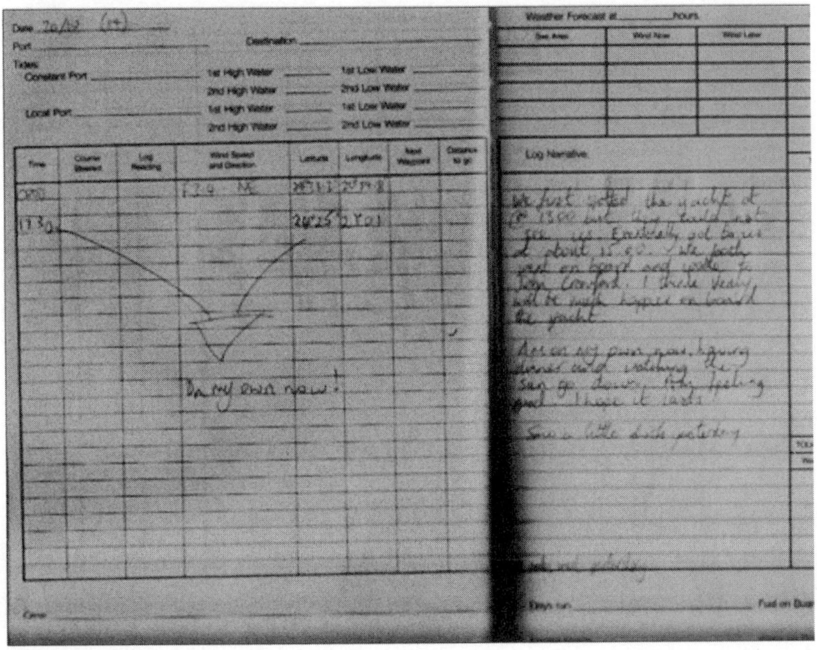

Monday January 28 Leading Article in *The Times*

QUEEN OF THE HIGH SEAS
A transatlantic heroine makes landfall

A low moan stole across the waters of the Atlantic last night. The Nereids sighed and dropped their lovely heads – not since Thetis's departure had they lost such a sister. Poseidon lulled wretchedly about his kingdom, wistfully caressing his beard. Not since his tussle with Athene had he relished such a contest. His horses tossed their manes. Where would they find such a racing companion? Only Aphrodite looked relieved, arms folded, eyeing the Barbados shore-line and a touching reunion between husband and wife. Hasn't she had enough problems with mermaids over the years without the addition of a golden-haired human speeding naked across the water? After 112 days watching a love affair between a mortal and the deep, there was one place she wanted Ms Debra Veal and that was back on land.

She got her wish. The Ward Evans Atlantic Rowing Challenge is over, and the winner is the contestant who came last. After more than three months at sea, Debra Veal – businesswoman, maritime nudist and consumer of more beef stew than a human should have to face – was lifted out of her craft by the husband who abandoned her to a lone quest. Onlookers went wild, tears and champagne flowed, and our heroine found that sea legs would not easily convert to landlubber limbs. And unlike the chaps who preceded her, Ms Veal turned up looking spick and span with clean hair and outfit and a very impressive tan.

Also unlike the chaps she did it alone. Ward Evans competitors were supposed to row in pairs but not everyone could take the pressure of the open seas, Ms Veal's husband included. While other deserted partners, including *Times* man Jonathan Gornall, eventually renounced the solo quest, Debs rowed on with the indomitable spirit shown by the little red hen in the children's fairy tale. The men got angsty and existential. Ms Veal was in her element – row, row, rowing her boat gently 'cross the stream, bumping into turtles and laughing gaily whilst being slapped in the face by flying fish. Like the yachtswoman Ellen MacArthur, Ms Veal's journey was spiritual as much as physical, a stripping away of layers until she reached her self's inner core, an achievement that she describes as a state of grace.

No one knows what they will find when they set out on such an adventure, but Ms Veal has come away with the ultimate reward. Armchair mariners everywhere can draw inspiration from her voyage of self-discovery. As she toasted her boat, *Troika Transatlantic*, 'this lady, this very special lady', so we, in turn, salute her.

Index